The Landscape of the
BRONTËS

The Landscape of the
BRONTËS

ARTHUR POLLARD

With photographs by Simon McBride

E. P. DUTTON . NEW YORK

Frontispiece: Ponden Kirk. Looking down Ponden Clough with Haworth Moor on right.

Published in the United States by E. P. Dutton,
a division of NAL Penguin Inc.,
2 Park Avenue, New York, N.Y. 10016.

Originally published in Great Britain by Webb & Bower (Publishers)
Limited in association with Michael Joseph Limited.

Library of Congress Catalog Card Number: 87 — 51115

ISBN: 0-525-24637-1

OBE

Designed by Vic Giolitto

1 3 5 7 9 10 8 6 4 2

First American Edition

Contents

Preface

A landscape ceases to be merely topographical when there are people in it. When those people are the Brontë sisters, the landscape is far more than topographical. It becomes a literary landscape, but the literature cannot be fully appreciated without the topography nor, in the case of these sisters, something of their biography. To understand their books we need to know their lives; to understand their lives we need to know where they were spent. The Brontë novels are redolent of the moors that roll away from the bleak upland manufacturing village of Haworth which has become world famous because it was there that these sad sisters and remarkable women passed their days.

In the text that follows I have drawn freely on illustrative passages from the novels and, as every writer on the Brontës must, I have called Charlotte's first and finest biographer, Mrs Gaskell, frequently to my aid. These provide the verbal foundation, Simon McBride's photography the memorable superstructure.

He and I would wish to acknowledge the help we have received, notably from the Council of the Brontë Society, who allowed us liberal access to their treasures; from Dr Juliet Barker, the Librarian of the Brontë Parsonage Museum, whose deep acquaintance with the subject both extended our own knowledge and brought to light new material for this volume; from her colleague, Sally Johnson; and, above all else, from Christine Sumner who gave generously of her time and her unrivalled familiarity with Brontëana detail not only to enable us to share her enthusiasm but also to save this work from inadequacies and error. Needless to say, whatever of these remain must be the responsibility of the author. I should like once again to thank Ruth Green for her immaculate deciphering of my execrable hand.

ARTHUR POLLARD

Introduction: The Brontë Legend

Shakespeare tells us that 'a sad tale's best for winter': so perhaps winter's best for a sad tale. On her first visit to Haworth Mrs Gaskell came not in winter but in late September, and even then 'It was a dull, drizzly Indian-inky day ... lead-coloured.' On her way she passed ' ... grey dull-coloured rows of stone-cottages ... poor, hungry-looking fields; stone-fences everywhere, and trees nowhere. Haworth is a long, straggling village: one steep narrow street ...' and when she reached the parsonage front door, '... moors everywhere beyond and above. The crowded grave-yard surrounds the house.' (*Life of Charlotte Brontë*, hereafter referred to as *Life*, Chapter 27) The modern visitor will recognize the scene—and the atmosphere.

Why then does he or she and thousands of others come to Haworth? 'To strangers ... who are unacquainted with the locality, ... to whom the inhabitants, the customs ... are things alien and familiar. To all such', Charlotte Brontë wrote in her preface to Emily's *Wuthering Heights*, 'the wild moors of the north of England can for them have no interest.' How wrong she has proved to be!

The reason for her error is the legend which she herself (and Emily) played such a large part in creating, so that what she called:

> ' ... no other landscape than a monotonous street—of moorland, a grey church tower, rising from the centre of a churchyard so filled with graves that the rank weed and coarse grass scarce had room to shoot up between the monuments ...'
>
> (*Roe Head Journal* 1831–2)

is the ordinary, but also one of the most extraordinary, literary landscapes in the world.

The sisters – Anne, Emily and Charlotte – as painted by their brother, Branwell. The 'pillar' space in this picture (now in the National Portrait Gallery) has been shown by infra-red photography to have been originally occupied by a male figure, probably Branwell himself. 'Emily's countenance struck me as full of power; Charlotte's of solicitude; Anne's of tenderness' (Mrs Gaskell's *Life*, Chapter 7)

The Brontës have fascinated biographers and literary critics from their day to ours and will go on doing so. How did those three apparently unremarkable sisters living a retired life in Haworth succeed in producing the memorable works that bear their names? That question is asked with greater pathos but also with greater certainty of answer when one remembers the circumstances of their lives. Out of their own suffering they portrayed suffering.

The Brontës

a family history

THE TREE

The Brontës are the most famous literary family in England. The novels of the three sisters, Charlotte, Emily and Anne, have been translated world wide and together with the story of their lives have inspired hundreds of books, films and plays. This international fame is all the more remarkable because the sisters lived most of their secluded lives in this house in the remote village of Haworth.

Hugh Brunty

Eleanor McClory
(Alice)

married 1776

Thomas Branwell
born 1746
died 5.4.1808

Anne Carne
baptised 27.4.1744
died 19.12.1809

married

Patrick Brontë
(Brunty)

married 29.12.1812

born 17.3.1777
died 7.6.1861

Maria Branwell
born 15.4.1783
died 15.9.1821

Elizabeth Branwell
(Aunt Branwell)
born 1776
died 1842

Maria
born 1814
died 6.5.1825

Elizabeth
born 8.2.1815
died 15.6.1825

Patrick Branwell
born 26.6.1817
died 24.9.1848

Emily Jane
born 30.7.1818
died 19.12.1848

Anne
born 17.1.1820
died 28.5.1849

Arthur Bell Nicholls

married 29.6.1854

born 1818
died 3.12.1906

Charlotte

born 21.4.1816
died 31.3.1855

The family tree, showing the Celtic ancestry of the sisters, father Irish and mother Cornish.

Mrs Gaskell, to whom we shall always owe the greatest debt both for our knowledge of, and sympathy with, the Brontës, found their story almost unbearable when she first heard it. Coming to know Charlotte well in the last five years of the latter's life, she had no hesitation in accepting the commission to write her biography. In recounting that history she was moved both to pity and indignation as she recalled what those sisters had gone through. Her information may not always have been accurate. It may, however, have been truer than either she or we can ever prove. Mr Brontë, after reading the work, eventually protested against its account of his eccentricities, but if Mary Taylor, Charlotte's friend, had cared to tell more than she did and Mrs Gaskell had dared to print it, he would have come out worse than he did. And, whatever the truth about the girls' experience at school at Cowan Bridge and whatever the truth about Branwell's association with Mrs Robinson, the narration of both of which experiences brought threats of legal action on Mrs Gaskell's head, there is no doubt that what she said the Brontës themselves thought to be the truth. There can therefore be no questioning of the emotional effects that those events had upon them.

Then, given their motherless condition and the isolation of their lives

Haworth Moors under snow
– a scene familiar to and
loved by the Brontë sisters.

in that grey parsonage, thrown intensely upon themselves and with those vivid imaginations, deriving from their Celtic ancestry, quickly expressing themselves, the sisters fascinate by their unusual condition of heredity, environment and action. The products of that background from their early years—the so-called 'little writings'—are known about but not widely read. But who needs these when we have that terrible portrayal of the passions which came from Emily, imaginatively the strongest of them all and as unsparing of herself as the characters she delineated? Charlotte recognized the massive achievement and the massive effort it had required. Speaking still of her sister as a man under the pseudonym 'Ellis Bell', she wrote in the 1850 Preface:

> '*Wuthering Heights* was hewn in a wild workshop, with simple tools, out of homely materials. The statuary found a granite block on a solitary moor: gazing thereon, he saw how from the crag might be elicited the head, savage, swart, sinister; a form moulded with at least one element of grandeur—power.'

That power makes *Wuthering Heights* unique among novels. It asks us to go through an experience that only the most terrifying drama requires. It has been, not unaptly, compared with *King Lear*.

The mid nineteenth-century reviewers were uncomfortable with both *Wuthering Heights* and *Jane Eyre*. Even *Agnes Grey* with its candid portrayal of the lot of governesses also touched too tender a spot for some of them, whilst Anne's other novel, *The Tenant of Wildfell Hall*, was much too explicit in describing the ravages of alcohol. The reviewers called them 'vulgar' novels. None of these works knows compromise or understatement. In consequence, the mainly middle-class readers were uneasy—forced to recognize but unable to fit the impression of the novels into the pattern of their own experience, standards or expectations. Lockwood in *Wuthering Heights*, that rather effete Southerner, who, like the ancient mariner, has to tell the strange story he has heard, is in a way symbolic of that readership—profoundly disturbed by what he saw, unable to measure it, wishing he had never got mixed up in it, but yet fascinated and compelled by it.

Nobody before had written like the Brontës; nobody since has written like them. In due time it was revealed that nobody had lived like them. Out of their books and their lives the Brontë legend took its birth.

1. Patrick Brontë Comes to Yorkshire

In December 1809 the Reverend John Buckworth, Vicar of Dewsbury, obtained a new curate. He was the Reverend Patrick Brontë, who had already served in that capacity first to Joseph Jowett, Professor of Civil Law at Cambridge and non-resident vicar of Wethersfield (Essex), and then briefly at Wellington (Shropshire) where he met William Morgan, a fellow curate, and John Fennell, a local headmaster, who were both to figure later in the Brontë story.

Patrick Brontë had come a long way to Dewsbury—from Drumbally-roney, in fact, an Irish village sheltering beneath the Mountains of Mourne. He was the eldest of ten children, born on St Patrick's Day (17 March) 1777, precocious son of a peasant farmer, Brunty (or even Prunty). Patrick was apprenticed to a blacksmith, worked as a linen weaver, and by the time he was sixteen had taken up teaching, shortly to be engaged as tutor by Thomas Tighe, vicar of Drumgooland. This was the time of the Evangelical Revival with its emphasis on fervent personal religious commitment. Tighe was a Protestant, so was Patrick. Tighe had known and been influenced by John Wesley. Tighe saw Patrick Brunty's potential and was instrumental in getting him to Cambridge, a journey, it is said, that, apart from the sea-crossing, Patrick undertook entirely on foot.

That was in September 1802 and on 1 October his name was duly entered as 'Patrick Branty' in the books of St John's College, Cambridge. What a transformation—from the poverty of peasant surroundings in his homeland to the venerable cloisters of an ancient university! Two days later Patrick changed the registration from 'Branty' to 'Bronte', which progressively moved to 'Bronté' and then 'Brontë'. From Irish brogue to Italian overtones! And was not the most celebrated sailor of the day, Lord Nelson, also Duke of Brontë?

Mist and loneliness:
Warley Moor above
Luddendenfoot.
'I dream of moor, and misty
hill,
Where evening closes dark
and chill'
Emily Brontë,
'The winter wind . . .'

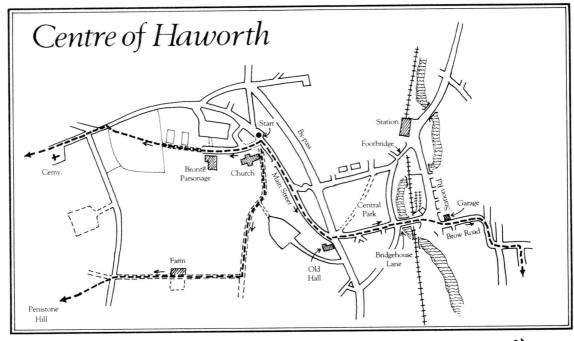

Centre of Haworth

Start

By-pass

Station

Footbridge

Station Rd.

Garage

Central Park

Brow Road

Bridgehouse Lane

Cemy.

Brontë Parsonage

Church

Main Street

Old Hall

Farm

Penistone Hill

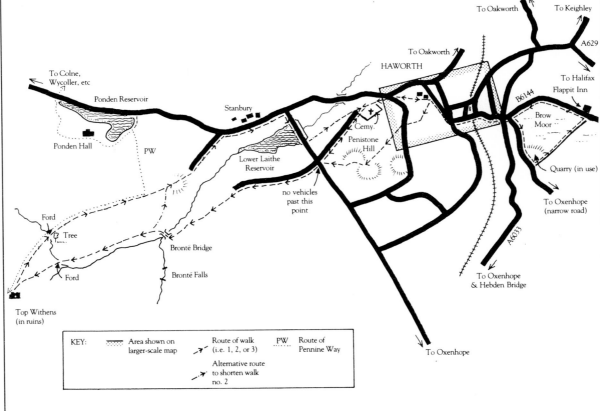

To Oakworth

To Keighley

A629

To Oakworth

HAWORTH

To Halifax

Flappit Inn

B6144

To Colne, Wycoller, etc

Ponden Reservoir

Stanbury

Cemy.

Brow Moor

Ponden Hall

PW

Penistone Hill

Quarry (in use)

Lower Laithe Reservoir

no vehicles past this point

To Oxenhope (narrow road)

Ford

Tree

A6033

Brontë Bridge

Brontë Falls

Ford

To Oxenhope & Hebden Bridge

Top Withens (in ruins)

To Oxenhope

KEY:
- Area shown on larger-scale map
- Route of walk (i.e. 1, 2, or 3)
- PW Route of Pennine Way
- Alternative route to shorten walk no. 2

The determination that had brought Patrick to Cambridge saw him through Cambridge. He was a sizar, that is, a poor student in receipt of college assistance—a Hare Exhibition and a Duchess of Suffolk Exhibition, in return for which he was required to perform various menial and coaching duties. In addition to this help he also received assistance from the Church Missionary Society—twenty pounds per year, but coming, in fact, from those two renowned Evangelical notables, Henry Thornton and William Wilberforce. Patrick graduated BA in April 1806 and was ordained in August of that year.

If Cambridge was such a change after Ireland, Dewsbury after Wethersfield and even after Wellington must have been as great a shock. From the sleepy rural south of the Essex countryside where he had met and jilted Mary Burder, Patrick Brontë came to a busy woollen district where looms rattled for more hours of the day than they were still. He came to an area where factories and cottages had sprung up in unplanned profusion in the eighteenth century, of which in 1757 with somewhat wry perspective the minor poet John Dyer could speak thus:

> 'Behold, in Calder's vale, where wide around
> Unnumber'd villas creep the shrubby hills . . . .
> The sprightly scene, where many a busy hand,
> Where spoles, cards, wheels and looms, with motion quick,
> And ever murmuring sound, th'unwonted sense
> Wrap in surprise . . . . The younger hands
> Ply at the easy work of winding yarn
> On swiftly circling engines, and their notes
> Warble together, as a choir of larks . . . .
> . . . Take we now our eastward course
> To the rich fields of Burstal. Wide around,
> Hillock and valley, farm and village smile,
> And ruddy roofs, and chimney tops appear,
> Of busy Leeds, up-wafting to the clouds
> The incense of thanksgiving.'

(The Fleece, Book III)

It is highly unlikely that the inhabitants themselves regarded the smoke-laden atmosphere in quite such terms. Nor was pollution the only problem. The introduction of new machinery—and with it the possible displacement of labour, especially that of the croppers[1]—led to the Luddite riots of 1811–12. Charlotte Brontë was to make these central to the action of *Shirley*, and no doubt what she wrote then owed much to what she had learned from her father of that time and those events.

[1] Croppers cut the nap off cloth with large shears. One machine could do the work of ten men operating by hand.

St Peter's Church, Hartshead, Patrick Brontë's first independent charge, stands high on the moor, some four miles from what was then its 'mother'-church at Dewsbury. One of his predecessors there had been Hammond Roberson, a truly militant Evangelical.

West Yorkshire was a stronghold of Anglican Evangelicalism. Henry Venn, saintly pioneer of the movement, had been vicar of Huddersfield. The Elland Society—then, and later, a gathering of like-minded clergy—served as a means of fellowship for the Evangelicals of the area. In Dewsbury itself Matthew Powley had preceded John Buckworth as vicar. Prominent also over forty years in the area was another Evangelical, Hammond Roberson, one of Patrick's predecessors at Dewsbury and Hartshead, who was to be portrayed in Charlotte's *Shirley*.

From ministering at the parish church of Dewsbury Patrick Brontë moved to the curacy of Hartshead where, after protracted preliminaries, he was inducted in July 1811. He had moved up the hill out of the valley of the Calder which runs through Dewsbury and which was probably then and was certainly later the filthiest river in England. At Hartshead he ministered in the ancient parish church of St Peter for three years.

What was Patrick Brontë like in these years? We are accustomed to envisage the old man of stern, even gloomy, appearance from the well-known portrait; and from the impression conveyed by Mrs Gaskell we

The Old Bell Chapel, Thornton was a plain rectangular building, its only decoration the small octagonal bell-tower still to be seen among the ruins. Inside, like so many churches before so-called Victorian restorations, including Haworth itself, it had three-decker pulpit and box pews. Five of the Brontë children were baptized here.

get a sense of his idiosyncratic and irascible behaviour. One who knew some who were able to recall the curate of Dewsbury and Hartshead records that 'he was noted for his winning way with children, and for his stiff manner with the *nouveaux riches*.' (J A Erskine Stuart, *The Brontë Country*, 1888, p 33) He was powerfully built and a 'very handsome fellow, full of Irish enthusiasm, and with something of an Irishman's capability of falling easily in love.' (*Life,* Chapter 3) Patrick Brontë did fall in love—with Maria Branwell, a Cornish girl from Penzance, who was staying with her aunt and uncle, the Fennells, at Woodhouse Grove School, Apperley Bridge, near Bradford. Patrick had gone there in June 1812 with his former Wellington colleague, William Morgan, now curate of Bradford Parish Church, who was engaged to Jane Fennell. We know all too little of Maria Brontë, but what she went through in the remaining years of her short life evokes our sympathies. She came of a Calvinistic Methodist family but, though the severity of that persuasion is said to have been displayed by her sister, Elizabeth, the Brontë children's 'Aunt Branwell', no speck of its dark shadow has ever been associated with Maria. She was apparently, like her daughters, extremely small in build—'not pretty, but very elegant,' says Mrs Gaskell 'and always dressed with a quiet simplicity of taste which accorded well with her general character.' (*Life*, Chapter 3)

Maria was then about thirty and, as she put it, 'for some years I have been perfectly my own mistress, subject to no control whatever.' She goes on to note that her sisters, and even her mother, deferred to her superior wisdom, and immediately recognizes that this may seem boastful. She adds therefore:

> 'But you must consider that I do not boast of it. I have many times felt it a disadvantage, and although, I thank God, it has never led me into error, yet, in circumstances of uncertainty and doubt, I have deeply felt the want of a guide and instructor.'
>
> (*Life*, Chapter 3)

This comes from one of some nine of her surviving letters to Patrick Brontë. He showed them to Charlotte when she alone was left of all the children. Of them she commented in a letter to Ellen Nussey of 16 February 1850:

> 'The papers were yellow with time: . . . it was strange now to peruse the records of a mind whence my own sprang; and most strange, and at once sad and sweet, to find that mind of a truly fine, pure and elevated order . . . . There is a rectitude, a constancy, a modesty, a sense, a gentleness about them indescribable. I wished that she had lived, and that I had known her . . . .'

The birthplace at Thornton, Patrick Brontë's second living. In this unimposing terraced house, built in 1802, were born Charlotte, Branwell, Emily and Anne.

The letters show more than that, however. They show the liveliness and happiness of her brief courtship with her dear 'saucy Pat'. Patrick Brontë and Maria Branwell were married in a double ceremony with William Morgan and Jane Fennell at Guiseley Parish Church on 29 December 1812, each bridegroom officiating at the marriage of the other couple.

The Brontës set up house at Clough Lane, Hightown, below the heights of Hartshead and on the way to Dewsbury. They went there in January 1813; their eldest daughter, Maria, was born there in January 1814, and their second daughter, Elizabeth, in February 1815. A month later Patrick exchanged the living of Hartshead for that of Thornton (near Bradford), where the remaining Brontë children were born—Charlotte (21 April 1816), Patrick Branwell (26 June 1817), Emily Jane (30 July 1818) and Anne (17 January 1820). The family moved to Haworth in April 1820 and within eighteen months Maria Brontë was dead of cancer. Her last words were, 'Oh, God, my poor children—oh, God, my poor children.'

This ill-fortuned family had suffered its first cruel blow. Patrick was left with these six children, the eldest merely seven years of age. The stricken father with what even in his circumstances may appear consummate haste proposed marriage to Anne's godmother, Elizabeth Firth of Thornton—and was rejected. In 1823 he turned to his old love, Mary Burder of Wethersfield. But hell hath no fury like a woman scorned and all Patrick got for his trouble was a letter in which Miss Burder thanked God for a lucky escape, or to put it in hers and the language of the time:

> 'This review, Sir, excites in my bosom increased gratitude and thankfulness to that wise, that indulgent Providence which then watched over me for good and withheld me from forming in very early life an indissoluble engagement with one whom I cannot think was altogether clear of duplicity.'

With what Margaret Lane in *The Brontë Story* (1969 edn p 48) has described as 'pious nastiness' Miss Burder concludes of Patrick's and his family's afflicted condition: 'The Lord can supply all your and their need.' Thus Mary Burder passes out of the Brontë story, some years later to become Mrs Sibree.

And so Patrick Brontë settled down to forty long years of widowerhood—with Elizabeth Branwell, his wife's sister ('Aunt Branwell'), to care for the growing family and to remain in residence at Haworth until her own death in 1842. This elder spinster sister of Maria Brontë seems to have had none of the warmth or charm that had so obviously attracted Patrick to the younger woman. She responded nobly

Elizabeth, 'Aunt Branwell', a silhouette of unknown date. She was Maria Brontë's older sister, and, despite her forbidding character, looked after the motherless Brontës for the rest of her life punctiliously.

to the needs of Patrick Brontë and his stricken family, but there is never any suggestion that she liked it or that they much liked her. Certainly the servants did not. Nancy Garrs, who helped to nurse the children, complained that Aunt Branwell was:

> '. . . so crosslike and fault-findin' and so close, she ga'e us, my sister Sarah and me, but a gill of beer a day, and she gi'e it hessel', did Miss Branwell, to our dinner, she wouldn't let us go draw it oursel' in t' cellar. A pint a day she gi'e us, that were half a pint for me an' half a pint for Sarah.'
> (Helen H Arnold 'The Reminiscences of Emma Huidekoper Cortazzo: A friend of Ellen Nussey', *Brontë Society Transactions*, 1958, Vol 13)

That was before Methodism got itself enmeshed with teetotal allegiances, or they might have had to be content with less appetizing beverages.

But if there were those in Yorkshire who liked Aunt Branwell but

Wellington Parish Church, a plain classical building with Norman-type apse,
erected in 1790 and therefore quite new in Patrick Brontë's time as curate there.
Nearby was the town of Madeley, famous in Evangelical circles by the presence
of John Fletcher, whose widow is said to have recommended Patrick Brontë for a
curacy at Dewsbury.

Opposite above
Marsh Top (near Haworth).

Opposite below
Dewsbury Parish Church, where Patrick Brontë first ministered as curate to the
then vicar, John Buckworth. An ancient building with Saxon relics and medieval
glass, it was heavily restored in the 1880s. One of the main centres in Yorkshire of
Anglican Evangelicalism in the late eighteenth and early nineteenth centuries.

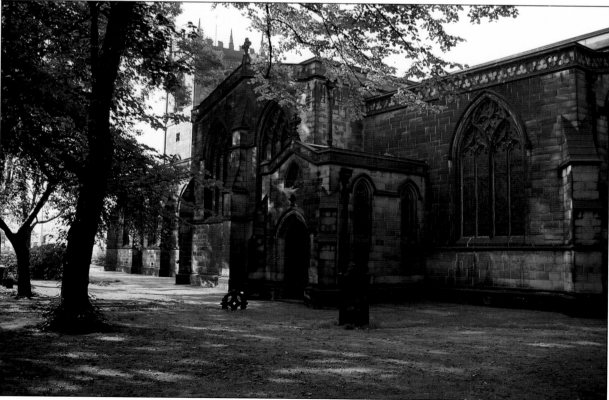

Haworth Moor – a characteristic landscape with rough tussocky grass, uneven dry stone walls, gaunt lone tree and solitary building.

little, she in her turn had no love for Yorkshire. After Cornwall she found Haworth, according to Mrs Gaskell:

'. . . a place where neither flowers nor vegetables would flourish, and where a tree of even moderate dimensions might be hunted for far and wide; where the snow lay long and late on the moors, stretching bleakly and barely far up from the dwelling which was henceforward to be her home; and where often, on autumnal or winter nights, the four winds of heaven seemed to meet and rage together, tearing round the house as if they were wild beasts striving to find an entrance. She missed the small round of cheerful, social visiting perpetually going on in a country town; she missed the friends she had known from her childhood, some of whom had been her parents' friends before they were hers; she disliked many of the customs of the place, and particularly dreaded the cold damp arising from the flag floors in the passages and parlours of Haworth Parsonage.'

(*Life*, Chapter 4)

Nevertheless, in conformity with her stern faith, she buckled down to what she regarded as her duty and imposed her discipline upon the domestic economy that had fallen to her care. Besides supervising the servants she instructed the children in sewing and religion. This she did from her bedroom where she seems to have spent most of her time in strict isolation. Her régime moved with military precision, and of its later years Mrs Gaskell has recorded:

'People in Haworth have assured me that, according to the hour of day—nay, the very minute—could they have told what the inhabitants of the parsonage were about. At certain times the girls would be sewing in their aunt's bedroom—the chamber which, in former days, before they had outstripped her in their learning, had served them as a school-room; at certain (early) hours they had their meals; from six to eight, Miss Branwell read aloud to Mr Brontë; at punctual eight, the household assembled to evening prayers in his study; and by nine he, Miss Branwell, and Tabby, were all in bed.'

(*Life*, Chapter 8)

Opposite
St John's College, Cambridge from the Backs with the River Cam in the foreground. Patrick Brontë studied here from 1802–6 and here Wordsworth before him had looked on:
'Gowns grave or gaudy, doctors, students, streets,
Courts, cloisters, flocks of churches, gateways, towers.'
The Prelude (1850) III, 32–33
The 'Bridge of Sighs' was not built until 1831.

Mary Taylor called her 'a very precise person'.

Anne, perhaps because she was most amenable, seems to have been Aunt Branwell's favourite. She certainly imbibed, most obviously, some of that dreary Calvinism that marked her aunt's beliefs. In a poem addressed 'To Cowper', that ultimate Calvinist in that he believed he had been specifically elected to damnation, she wrote:

> 'The language of my inmost heart
>   I traced in every line
> *My* sins, *my* sorrows, hopes, and fears
>   Were there—and only mine . . . .
>
> [And] should thy darkest fears be true,
>   If Heaven be so severe,
> That such a soul as thine is lost,—
>   Oh! how shall I appear?'

Charlotte, too, experienced a phase of Calvinistic anxiety around 1836, but both she and Anne passed through it safely. Their later theological position, as far as one can define it, seems indeed to be at the opposite end of the spectrum. They both embraced some sort of belief in universal salvation for all mankind.

Opposite above
View from the moors with Haworth in the middle distance. The village remains today much the same size as in the time of the Brontës.

Opposite below
Woodhouse Grove School where Patrick Brontë first met his future wife Maria Branwell, when he was visiting to examine the boys in religious education.

2. Haworth and the Parsonage

The Brontës' move from Thornton to Haworth was a move into bleaker country, up the hills and onto the moors of this outcrop of the Pennine Chain. Two miles they climbed from Thornton up to Denholme, the removal carts proceeding slowly on their way. Even in summer this road has a cheerless atmosphere, passing as it does through tracts of rough, bare sheep pasture. In winter it is reminiscent of the lands from which the Scandinavian settlers in the area had come—with plenty of snow; and that still lying when it has long disappeared from the fields below. It is land where the predominant colour for much of the year is not green, but dun brown and black, save when in summer the moors bloom purple with heather. That way the family came, as the traveller from Bradford still does who comes to Haworth, though nowadays in far greater comfort than was theirs. Abraham Holroyd, an early commentator, described the Brontë migration:

> 'Hour after hour passes, and they leave Old Allen, Flappit Spring and Braemoor behind, and late in the afternoon the inhabitants of the quiet village of Haworth behold them pass up their steepest of all streets, and halt at the door of the parsonage. Thus came the Brontës to Haworth, strangers among strangers.'
> (*Currer Bell and Her Sisters*, 1887)

Characteristically, in the railway age Mrs Gaskell approached Haworth from another direction. Beginning her work on *The Life of Charlotte Brontë*, just after her friend and fellow novelist had died, she travelled by train from Manchester to Keighley and thence by road to Haworth. This was her impression:

The parsonage and the school seen from
the churchyard in winter.

'For two miles the road passes over tolerably level ground, distant
hills on the left, a 'beck' flowing through meadows on the right, and
furnishing water power, at certain points, to the factories built on its
banks. The air is dim and lightless with the smoke from all these
habitations and places of business. The soil in the valley (or
'bottom', to use the local term) is rich; but, as the road begins to
ascend, the vegetation becomes poorer; it does not flourish, it
merely exists; and, instead of trees, there are only bushes and shrubs
about the dwellings. Stone dykes are everywhere used in place of
hedges; and what crops there are, on the patches of arable land,
consist of pale, hungry-looking, grey-green oats. Right before the
traveller on this road rises Haworth village; he can see it for two
miles before he arrives, for it is situated on the side of a pretty steep
hill, with a background of dun and purple moors, rising and
sweeping away yet higher than the church, which is built at the very
summit of the long narrow street. All round the horizon there is this
same line of sinuous wave-like hills; the scoops into which they fall
only revealing other hills beyond, of similar colour and shape,
crowned with wild, bleak moors—grand, from the ideas of solitude

Haworth main street with its steep cobbled surface.

Old alleyway off Haworth main street.

and loneliness which they suggest, or oppressive from the feeling which they give of being pent-up by some monotonous and illimitable barrier, according to the mood of mind in which the spectator may be.'

(Life, Chapter 2)

How Mr Brontë came to find himself in Haworth is a story in itself. The census for 1821 records the inhabitants of this 'populous manufacturing village' as numbering 4668. They were a sturdy, independent, self-willed people, men who compelled the surroundings to yield them a living. To Mrs Gaskell who, though she had her 'Cranford' upbringing behind her, nonetheless knew the plain outspoken ways of Manchester workingmen, these West Riding folk were a :

> ' . . . wild, rough population. Their accost is curt; their accent and tone of speech is blunt and harsh . . . . Their feelings are not easily roused, but their duration is lasting. Hence there is much close friendship and faithful service . . . . From the same cause come also enduring grudges, in some cases amounting to hatred, which occasionally has been bequeathed from generation to generation.'

(Life, Chapter 2)

The presentation to the perpetual curacy of Haworth was full of acrimonious potential and in 1819 potential became actuality. The right of presentation lay with the vicar of Bradford, but the funds on which the clergyman's stipend largely depended were in the hands of local trustees who staunchly maintained their right not just to veto but even, it seems, to nominate. They turned away Patrick Brontë because he was the vicar of Bradford's choice, so then the vicar sent them Samuel Redhead who was somewhat less prudent than the Irishman the inhabitants of Haworth had first rejected and who then came to spend the rest of his life amongst them.

On his first appearance Redhead officiated in a full church or, more accurately, he began to do so, for at the beginning of the second lesson he was faced by a mass exit of the congregation, all clog-shod and 'clattering and clumping'. Next Sunday there was a variation of the resistance. Halfway through the service, face to tail and wearing several old hats, a man rode into church and round the aisles on a donkey. Screams, laughter and general pandemonium—and the premature end of yet another service. The persistent parson tried again, this time accompanied by friends from Bradford. The parishioners brought with them a soot-begrimed and drunken chimneysweep. 'They placed him right before the reading-desk, where his blackened face nodded a drunken, stupid assent

Samuel Redhead, the cleric so mistreated
by the parishioners of Haworth, later
became vicar of Calverley.

to all that Mr Redhead said.' (*Life*, Chapter 2) The climax came when the
sweep ascended the stairs of the old three-decker pulpit and embraced the
surprised cleric, black as the devil against the white of the surplice. To
complete the débâcle, the parishioners pursued the retreating pair out of
the church, hurled both of them into the soot the sweep had deposited,
and Redhead with his friends escaped not only further insult but also
possible serious injury by seeking refuge in the nearby Black Bull Inn.
That was the end of Samuel Redhead, so far as Haworth was concerned,
except that he did return to preach several years later when all trace of
malice had disappeared from both sides. Patrick Brontë came into his
own, acceptable to the independent parishioners of Haworth because of
his more circumspect behaviour towards them than had been that of his
would-be replacement.

So Patrick entered into residence at Haworth Parsonage and into
ministry at the church of St Michael and All Angels (not St Autest, as Mrs
Gaskell so unaccountably called it). Let her, however, describe the
approach up the village street, for, though in essentials much survives,

Opposite
Haworth Church today and, *above*, Haworth Church in Patrick Brontë's time.
His successor considerably altered the church, as was the fashion at the time,
calling it 'restoration', in that the mid-Victorian passion was for Elizabethan and
medieval styles, becoming known as Victorian Gothic.

Haworth Church and Parsonage. The frontispiece to Vol II of Mrs Gaskell's *Life
of Charlotte Brontë*.

she herself must remain the most reliable guide to the scene as it was actually known to Charlotte Brontë and her sisters:

> 'For a short distance the road appears to turn away from Haworth, as it winds round the base of the shoulder of a hill; but then it crosses a bridge over the 'beck', and the ascent through the village begins. The flag-stones with which it is paved are placed end-ways, in order to give a better hold to the horses' feet; and, even with this help, they seem to be in constant danger of slipping backwards. The old stone houses are high compared to the width of the street, which makes an abrupt turn before reaching the more level ground at the head of the village, so that the steep aspect of the place, in one part, is almost like that of a wall. But this surmounted, the church lies a little off the main road on the left; a hundred yards, or so, and the driver relaxes his care, and the horse breathes more easily, as they pass into the quiet little by-street that leads to Haworth Parsonage. The church-yard is on one side of this lane, the school-house and the sexton's dwelling (where the curates formerly lodged) on the other.'
>
> (*Life*, Chapter 2)

The church and the parsonage are, nowadays, much altered from what they were in Brontë times. After the fashion of the period Patrick Brontë's successor, the Reverend John Wade, changed things in the name of restoration and the old church with its open 'old meeting-house' interior, box-pews and three-decker pulpit, disappeared altogether, apart from the tower. Simplicity gave way to decoration. Now there is a building, consisting of the nave with six bays, north and south aisles of five, the chancel of three and side chapels of two. One of these (that on the south side) is now given over to the Brontës. The ornateness of the church comes from the Derbyshire alabaster panel of Da Vinci's *Last Supper* above the holy table, and the accompanying pulpit, font and altar screen made from the same material. As for the parsonage, it was doubtless too small for Mr Wade's needs and his extension has proved useful in accommodating exhibits since the house was taken over by the Brontë Society. The nice proportions of the original Georgian building are gone, but it is still possible with the mind's eye to imagine it without its Victorian excrescence.

Again Mrs Gaskell serves us well:

Opposite
The parsonage kitchen. Charlotte's 'History of the Year 1829' reads 'Tabby, the servant, is washing up the breakfast-things, and Anne, my youngest sister . . ., is kneeling on a chair, looking at some cakes which Tabby has been baking for us . . . Aunt is upstairs in her room, and I am sitting by the table writing this in the kitchen.'

Above
Mr Brontë's study with his portrait on the wall. Haworth Parsonage, now the
Brontë Museum, contains Brontë clothes and furniture, and incorporates the
Bonnell Collection, put together over thirty years by Henry Houston Bonnell of
Philadelphia.

Opposite above
The sitting-room in the parsonage with Richmond's portrait of Charlotte over
the mantelpiece.

Opposite below
Items on Charlotte's desk – steel pens did not come into use until the 1860s,
fountain pens in the 1890s.

The Black Bull Hotel by the church steps – a favourite haunt of Branwell's.

'The parsonage stands at right angles to the road, facing down upon the church; so that, in fact, parsonage, church and belfried schoolhouse, form three sides of an irregular oblong, of which the fourth is open to the fields and moors that lie beyond. The area of this oblong is filled up by a crowded churchyard, and a small garden or court in front of the clergyman's house. As the entrance to this from the road is at the side, the path goes round the corner into the little plot of ground. Underneath the windows is a narrow flower-border, carefully tended in days of yore, although only the most hardy plants could be made to grow there. Within the stone wall, which keeps out the surrounding churchyard, are bushes of elder and lilac; the rest of the ground is occupied by a square grass plot and a gravel walk. The house is of grey stone, two stories high, heavily roofed with flags, in order to resist the winds that might strip off a lighter covering. It appears to have been built about a hundred years ago, and to consist of four rooms on each story; the two windows on the right (as the visitor stands, with his back to the

Opposite above
The parsonage viewed from the churchyard, with the Victorian extension on the right largely obscured by trees.

Above
Stained glass windows at Haworth Parsonage, originally in the
back parlour of Red House, Gomersal.

Left
The churchyard from the parsonage windows.
'I see around me piteous tombstones grey
Stretching their shadows far away.'

       Emily Brontë, 'I see around me . . .'

Haworth viewed from the quarry between the village and the moor; this is how the sisters would have seen the church when returning from a moorland walk.

Above
Church Lane, Haworth, and
the school on the right where
Charlotte instructed the
children of Haworth in the
Sunday School.

Haworth main street. Mrs
Gaskell wrote 'Haworth is
built with an utter disregard
of all sanitary conditions: the
great old churchyard lies
above all the houses, and it is
terrible to think how the very
water-springs of the pumps
below must be poisoned.'
(*Life*, Chapter 7) Not so
today, of course.

Haworth Church – unrestored interior with box pews and three-decker pulpit. This pulpit was the one used by Patrick Brontë's most famous predecessor, the 'Hell-fire' preacher William Grimshaw, who used to leave the church during the reading of the lessons to round up villagers who might be drinking in the nearby public houses.

church, ready to enter in at the front door) belonging to Mr Brontë's study, the two on the left to the family sitting-room. Everything about the place tells of the most dainty order, the most exquisite cleanliness. The door-steps are spotless; the small old-fashioned window-panes glitter like looking-glass. Inside and outside of that house cleanliness goes up into its essence, purity.'

(*Life*, Chapter 2)

We need to dwell longer on this building that housed such remarkable genius.[1] Entering the house, one has immediately on one's right the room which was Patrick Brontë's own special sanctum, usually called his study, and on the left the sitting-room. Ellen Nussey, Charlotte's closest friend from 1831 to her death, has recorded her impressions of the house at the time of her visit in 1833:

[1]For a detailed account see Jocelyn Kellett, *Haworth Parsonage: The Home of the Brontës*, Haworth, The Brontë Society, 1977.

Braemoor (or Browmoor) in winter, barren, empty and forbidding.
'We know where deepest lies the snow
And where the frost-winds blow,
On every mountain-brow'
Anne Brontë, 'Song'

'There was not much carpet anywhere except in the sitting-room, and on the study floor. The hall floor and stairs were done with sand-stone, always beautifully clean, as everything was about the house; the walls were not papered, but stained in a pretty dove-coloured tint; hair-seated chairs and mahogany tables, book-shelves in the study, but not many of these elsewhere. Scant and bare indeed, many will say, yet it was not a scantness that made itself felt. Mind and thought, I had almost said elegance, but certainly refinement, diffused themselves over all, and made nothing really wanting.'

('Reminiscences of Charlotte Brontë', *Scribner's Magazine*, 1871, Vol 2)

In the letter Mrs Gaskell quotes about the visit of the Winkworth sisters we are told that in the sitting-room they:

' . . . looked at a picture of Miss Brontë, by Richmond, the solitary ornament of the room, looking strangely out of place on the bare walls, and at the books on the little shelves, most of them evidently the gift of the authors since Miss Brontë's celebrity.'

(*Life*, Chapter 22)

That was in 1850 when there were still 'uncarpeted stone stairs and floors'. By 1853 an engraving of Lawrence's portrait of Thackeray had been added. Writing to thank George Smith for it, Charlotte added:

'For companion he has the Duke of Wellington (do you remember giving me that picture?) and for contrast and foil Richmond's portrait of an unworthy individual, who, in such society, must be nameless.'

Mrs Gaskell visited Haworth in September 1854. She tells of the domestic routine—of breakfast for Charlotte with her father in his study at nine, housework with the faithful ageing servant Tabby and the young girl during the morning, a walk, dinner at two, with Mr Brontë eating alone in his study, then rest and talk. She goes on to remark:

'It is a cold country, and the fires were a pretty warm dancing light all over the house. The parlour has evidently been refurnished within the last few years, since Miss Brontë's success has enabled her to have a little more money to spend. Everything fits into and is in harmony with, the idea of a country parsonage, possessed by people of very moderate means. The prevailing colour of the room is

Haworth under snow. The village is still frequently isolated in winter during heavy snowfalls. Its cobbled streets, designed to give the horses a grip as they climbed the steep hill, must in the Brontës' time have been truly impassable.

crimson, to make a warm setting for the cold grey landscape outside.'

(*Life*, Chapter 27)

The Richmond Brontë and the Lawrence Thackeray were still there, and the books neatly filling the two recesses on either side of the high, narrow, old-fashioned mantelpiece.

Mrs Gaskell was right about the refurnishing. It must have happened alongside the structural alterations—moving of walls, enlarging of rooms and the like, which Charlotte commissioned and which were carried out between May and July 1850 when she was on her travels to London, Birstall and Edinburgh but when her father was much less comfortably in residence. In the process of these alterations, too, Charlotte ordered William Wood, the Haworth joiner, 'to renew the furniture of the house from top to bottom, throughout with his own make.' She did not, however, discard the fine set of six late eighteenth-century chairs in Mr Brontë's study.

The small room on the left behind the dining-room/parlour was originally a storeroom entered from outside, as was the bedroom above, which served for many, many years to accommodate Tabby (Tabitha Aykroyd). When Charlotte married, the storeroom was converted and became a study for her husband, Arthur Bell Nicholls. A fireplace and outside chimney were built. Opposite this room was the kitchen, and underneath that the cellar where Aunt Branwell brewed the beer—and insisted on drawing it herself! Upstairs the room over Mr Brontë's study was his bedroom, that over the sitting-room was occupied by Aunt Branwell and later by Charlotte, and between the two was a small bedroom known as the nursery and later used by Emily. Over the kitchen was the room called Branwell's room. Beyond the house along a cold flagged passage was the back kitchen.

This was the Brontë home, cold and cheerless in the eyes of many, sad undoubtedly in the years of bereavement, but, if we are to accept the testimony of the sisters, a place where they found their own joy and happiness in the years they were together. Emily with her deep spiritual affinities with place could not leave the parsonage without quickly wanting, and having, to return. Gentle Anne, more long suffering, would yearn from her exiled governess post near York:

> 'Restore to me that little spot,
> With grey walls compassed round . . .
> Oh give me back my home!'

And, further away still, Charlotte in Brussels vividly imagined the lively Sunday morning scene at home with Emily and the dogs Tiger and Keeper more than interested in the preparation of the Sunday dinner.

3. Cowan Bridge

The Brontë children first left home in 1823 when the two eldest spent a few months at Crofton Hall School near Wakefield, from which they were removed apparently because the cost was too great. Patrick Brontë, with five motherless daughters, must have welcomed the establishment of the Clergy Daughters' School, charging the incredibly low fee of only fourteen pounds a year for both board and lodging.

This school opened on 30 January 1824 at Cowan Bridge, near Tunstall and Kirkby Lonsdale, on the road between Skipton and Kendal. It was the foundation of the wealthy Evangelical clergyman and landowner, William Carus Wilson, and in its support were such eminent 'godly' names as William Wilberforce, Hannah More and Charles Simeon. Thither went the two eldest Brontë children, Maria and Elizabeth, still weak after a winter of illness which had included chicken-pox, whooping-cough and measles. They were registered on 21 July, and thither also three weeks later by coach from Keighley, with her father, came Charlotte, to be joined in late November by Emily, who was to become the 'pet nursling' of the school.

Carus Wilson bought a row of eighteenth-century cottages, some seventy yards from the banks of the little River Leck, and converted these into the school dining-room, the Superintendent's lodging, and bed-rooms for the staff. At each end of the row he built a wing at right angles, one to house the schoolroom with four dormitories above it, the other a covered veranda for exercise in bad weather. Today only the cottages, reverted to their original use, are left. The rest of the building, after ceasing to be used as a school in 1833, was destroyed by fire during the Victorian period.

The staff consisted of six teachers, two under-teachers, a Super-intendent and six servants, together with a visiting music master.

Cowan Bridge School from the bridge over the River Leck.

Ominously in that staff list was Miss Finch, whose duties embraced 'Singing and Scourgemistress' and as the prospectus put it:

> ' . . . a lady well known for the pious fortitude and resignation with which she has borne various trying afflictions, who was engaged for a very trifling remuneration to assist me in regulating the *Discipline* of the College.'

She presumably derived satisfactions other than financial from her activities!

Charlotte has left us a memorable account of the Cowan Bridge experience in the Lowood chapters of *Jane Eyre*. The Leck valley can be quite beautiful and Charlotte so describes it in the first spring of Jane Eyre's sojourn at Lowood:

Opposite
Cowan Bridge: a view from the school with the little River Leck in spate.
Charlotte must often have thought that 'every prospect pleases and only man is vile'.

The Clergy Daughters' School, Cowan Bridge, as engraved by Jewitt of Derby in 1824. The two wings were later destroyed by fire. The girls were each given a small patch of garden to cultivate for themselves.

'I discovered, too, that a great pleasure, an enjoyment which the horizon only bounded, lay all outside the high and spike-guarded walls of our garden: this pleasure consisted in prospect of noble summits girdling a great hill-hollow rich in verdure and shadow: in a bright beck, full of dark stones and sparkling eddies. How different had this scene looked when I viewed it laid out beneath the iron sky of winter, stiffened in frost, shrouded with snow!—when mists as chill as death wandered to the impulse of east winds along those purple peaks, and rolled down "ing" and holm till they blended with the frozen fog of the beck! That beck itself was then a torrent, turbid and curbless: it tore asunder the wood, and sent a raving sound through the air, often thickened with wild rain or whirling sleet; and for the forest on its banks, *that* showed only ranks of skeletons.

April advanced to May: a bright, serene May it was; days of blue sky, placid sunshine, and soft western or southern gales filled up its duration. And now vegetation matured with vigour; Lowood shook loose its tresses; it became all green, all flowery; its great elm, ash, and oak skeletons were restored to majestic life; woodland plants sprang up profusely in its recesses; unnumbered varieties of moss filled its hollows, and it made a strange ground-sunshine out of the wealth of its wild primrose plants: I have seen their pale gold gleam in overshadowed spots like scatterings of the sweetest lustre.'

(*Jane Eyre*, Chapter 9)

But that comes after Jane's arrival in the depth of winter. Charlotte herself had arrived at Cowan Bridge in high summer. The different time of year which she chose for her heroine's coming to Lowood is just one of the ways in which she indicates her ineradicable dislike for this school, where she and her sisters suffered so much.

Speaking of the area for outdoor exercise, she wrote:

'The garden was a wide enclosure, surrounded with walls so high as to exclude every glimpse of prospect; a covered veranda ran down one side, and broad walks bordered a middle space divided into scores of little beds: these beds were assigned as gardens for the pupils to cultivate, and each bed had an owner. When full of flowers they would doubtless look pretty; but now, at the latter end of January, all was wintry blight and brown decay. I shuddered as I stood and looked round me. It was an inclement day for outdoor exercise; not positively rainy, but darkened by a drizzling yellow fog; all under foot was still soaking wet with the floods of yesterday. The stronger among the girls ran about and engaged in active games, but sundry pale and thin ones herded together for shelter and warmth in the veranda; and amongst these, as the dense mist penetrated to their shivering frames, I heard frequently the sound of a hollow cough.'

(*Jane Eyre*, Chapter 5)

The régime itself was harsh and the food was often intolerable. Mrs Gaskell describes it in detail, but some selections will suffice:

'Oatmeal porridge for breakfast; a piece of oat-cake for those who required luncheon; baked and boiled beef, and mutton, potato-pie, and plain homely puddings of different kinds for dinner. At five o'clock, bread and milk for the younger ones; and one piece of bread (this was the only time at which the food was limited) for the elder pupils, who sat up till a later meal of the same description. Mr Wilson himself ordered in the food, and was anxious that it should be of good quality. But the cook, who had much of his confidence, and against whom for a long time no one durst utter a complaint, was careless, dirty, and wasteful. To some children oatmeal porridge is distasteful, and consequently unwholesome, even when properly made; at Cowan Bridge School it was often sent up, not merely burnt, but with offensive fragments of other substances discovered in it. The beef, that should have been carefully salted before it was dressed, had often become tainted from neglect; and girls, who were schoolfellows with the Brontës, during the reign of the cook of whom I am speaking, tell me that the house seemed to be pervaded, morning, noon, and night, by the odour of rancid fat that steamed out of the oven in which much of their food was prepared. There was the same carelessness in making the puddings; one of those ordered was rice boiled in water, and eaten with a sauce of treacle and sugar; but it was often uneatable, because the water had been taken out of the rain-tub, and was strongly impregnated with the dust lodging on the roof, whence it had trickled down into the old wooden cask, which also added its own flavour to that of the original rain water. The milk, too, was often 'bingy', to use a country expression for a kind of taint that is far worse than sourness, and suggests the idea that it is caused by want of cleanliness about the milk pans, rather than by the heat of the weather. On Saturdays, a kind of pie, or mixture of potatoes and meat, was served up, which was made of all the fragments accumulated during the week. Scraps of meat from a dirty and disorderly larder, could never be very appetizing; and, I believe, that this dinner was more loathed than any in the early days of Cowan's Bridge School. One may fancy how repulsive such fare would be to children whose appetites were small, and who had been accustomed to food, far simpler perhaps, but prepared with a delicate cleanliness that made it both tempting and wholesome. Many a meal the little Brontës went without food, although craving with hunger.'

(*Life*, Chapter 4)

As if this were not bad enough, the suffering was compounded by the pietistic canting of Carus Wilson (as Brocklehurst) himself:

"'I find, in settling accounts with the housekeeper, that a lunch, consisting of bread and cheese, has twice been served out to the girls during the past fortnight. How is this? I looked over the regulations, and I find no such meal as lunch mentioned. Who introduced this innovation? and by what authority?"

"I must be responsible for the circumstance, sir," replied Miss Temple: "the breakfast was so ill prepared that the pupils could not possibly eat it; and I dared not allow them to remain fasting till dinner-time."

William Carus Wilson, a stern-faced portrait of the man who became the model
for Mr Brocklehurst in *Jane Eyre*.

"Madam, allow me an instant. You are aware that my plan in
bringing up these girls is, not to accustom them to habits of luxury
and indulgence, but to render them hardy, patient, self-denying.
Should any little accidental disappointment of the appetite occur,
such as the spoiling of a meal, the under or the over dressing of a
dish, the incident ought not to be neutralized by replacing with
something more delicate the comfort lost, thus pampering the body
and obviating the aim of this institution; it ought to be improved to
the spiritual edification of the pupils, by encouraging them to evince
fortitude under the temporary privation. A brief address on those
occasions would not be mistimed, wherein a judicious instructor
would take the opportunity of referring to the sufferings of the
primitive Christians; to the torments of the martyrs; to the

Tunstall Church where Charlotte and her sisters went with their fellow pupils each Sunday. The vicar was William Carus Wilson.

exhortations of our blessed Lord Himself, calling upon His disciples to take up their cross and follow Him; to His warnings that man shall not live by bread alone, but by every word that proceedeth out of the mouth of God; to His divine consolations, 'If ye suffer hunger or thirst for My sake, happy are ye.' Oh madam, when you put

Tunstall Church interior showing the loft over the doorway where the girls from Cowan Bridge School supposedly ate their lunch between morning and afternoon service. It could not have accommodated many at one time. 'The girls took their cold dinner with them and ate it between the services, in a chamber over the entrance opening out of the former galleries.' (Mrs Gaskell's *Life*)

bread and cheese, instead of burnt porridge, into these children's mouths, you may indeed feed their vile bodies, but you little think how you starve their immortal souls!"'

(*Jane Eyre*, Chapter 7)

Wilson was given to writing what he (and many other Victorians, be it said) regarded as edifying stories in which young children were happy to die because thereby they went to heaven and escaped the ills of earth. Surely Charlotte Brontë is engaging in mocking parody when she has Jane Eyre respond to Brocklehurst's cross-examination thus:

"'No sight so sad as that of a naughty child," he began, "especially a naughty little girl. Do you know where the wicked go after death?"
"They go to hell," was my ready and orthodox answer.
"And what is hell? Can you tell me that?"
"A pit full of fire."

"And should you like to fall into that pit, and to be burning there for ever?"

"No, sir."

"What must you do to avoid it?"

I deliberated a moment; my answer, when it did come, was objectionable: "I must keep in good health, and not die."'

(*Jane Eyre*, Chapter 4)

The girls of Cowan Bridge School had to go and listen to this man's real-life equivalent preaching in Tunstall Church each Sunday, over two miles across fields, flower bedecked and with trees rich in green foliage in summer, but in winter cold unsheltered country and very wet underfoot:

'Sundays were dreary days in that winter season. We had to walk two miles to Brocklebridge Church .... We set out cold, we arrived at church colder; during the morning service we became almost paralyzed. It was too far to return to dinner, and an allowance of cold meat and bread, in the same penurious proportion observed in our ordinary meals, was served round between the services.

At the close of the afternoon service we returned by an exposed and hilly road, where the bitter winter wind, blowing over a range of snowy summits to the north, almost flayed the skin from our faces.'

(*Jane Eyre*, Chapter 7)

Opposite above
Looking through the bow-windows of Roe Head as Charlotte must herself have done when she was there first as a pupil, then as teacher. This graceful Georgian house commands views as far as Kirklees Park and the attractive hills around Huddersfield; the same view her father had known at Hartshead.

Opposite below
Wycoller Hall, standing solitary and ruined beside its stream – a possible model for Ferndean in *Jane Eyre*. It stands only eight miles from Haworth, over the county border in Lancashire.

Above
Wath Church near Norton Conyers, where the Graham tombs are to be found.

The bridge at Wycoller, the possible model for Ferndean in *Jane Eyre*.
'Even within a very short distance of the manor house you could see nothing of it; so thick and dark grew the timber of the gloomy wood about it.' (*Jane Eyre*, Chapter 37)

Opposite
Bridlington, on Yorkshire's coast; the sweep of the bay where Charlotte first saw the sea, 'distant glimpses of the German Ocean.' Bridlington was to become a popular holiday resort.

(Legend has it that the children ate their meal in the still-existing little room above the porch in Tunstall Church.)

Nor was this all. There was also Miss Scatcherd, (based, it appears, not on the already mentioned Miss Finch but on a Miss Andrews), the fault-finding flogger whose chief victim was the angelic Helen Burns, fictional version of Charlotte's eldest sister, Maria, whom she adored and remembered long after she was dead. Persecuted as she was, Helen remained patient and uncomplaining and provided support for the much less long-suffering Jane. When, given the conditions under which these children lived, the inevitable epidemic arrived, as it did in real-life Cowan Bridge, Helen was struck down, as Maria Brontë was. She bore her illness with the same fortitude as she had borne Miss Scatcherd's persecution. Superficially (and ironically) there are parallels between the way in which Helen meets death with those of the pious children Carus Wilson wrote about, but by contrast with his emphasis on the destruction of those who failed to believe, Helen rested calmly in the belief that 'My Maker and yours will never destroy what He created. I rest implicitly on His power, and confide wholly in His goodness.' (*Jane Eyre*, Chapter 9)

If an informant of Mrs Gaskell is to be believed (and despite the threats of libel action she received, there is no reason why this statement

Opposite above
The estate of Norton Conyers, a fourteenth-century manor house, in the trees of which the rooks of *Jane Eyre* may have nested.

Opposite below
'Flower in the crannied wall' at Wycoller.
'A fine and subtle spirit dwells
In every little flower,
Each one its own sweet feeling breathes
With more or less of power'
Anne Brontë

Fields between Cowan Bridge and Tunstall over which the girls walked each Sunday, a circuitous path covering a distance of nearly three miles, often getting their feet wet and remaining cold and uncomfortable for the several hours they had to spend in Tunstall Church.

should not be), there was worse in the real 'Miss Scatcherd's' treatment of Maria than got into *Jane Eyre*:

> 'The dormitory in which Maria slept was a long room, holding a row of narrow little beds on each side, occupied by the pupils; and at the end of this dormitory there was a small bed-chamber opening out of it, appropriated to the use of Miss Scatcherd. Maria's bed stood nearest to the door of this room. One morning, after she had become so seriously unwell as to have had a blister applied to her side (the sore from which was not perfectly healed), when the getting-up bell was heard, poor Maria moaned out that she was so ill, so very ill, she wished she might stop in bed; and some of the girls urged her to do so, and said they would explain it all to Miss Temple, the superintendent. But Miss Scatcherd was close at hand, and her anger would have to be faced before Miss Temple's kind thoughtfulness could interfere; so the sick child began to dress, shivering with cold, as, without leaving her bed, she slowly put on her black worsted stockings over her thin white legs (my informant spoke as if she saw it yet, and her whole face flashed out undying indignation). Just then Miss Scatcherd issued from her room, and, without asking for a word of explanation from the sick and frightened girl, she took her by the arm, on the side to which the blister had been applied, and by one vigorous movement whirled her out into the middle of the floor, abusing her all the time for dirty and untidy habits. There she left her. My informant says, Maria hardly spoke, except to beg some of the more indignant girls to be calm; but, in slow, trembling movements, with many a pause, she went down stairs at last—and was punished for being late.'
>
> (*Life*, Chapter 4)

Maria might forgive, but Charlotte could never do so. She thought of her sister and Miss Scatcherd. Ellen Nussey recorded:

> '[Charlotte] described Maria as a little mother among the rest, superhuman in goodness and cleverness. But the most touching of all were the revelations of her sufferings—how she suffered with the sensibility of a grown-up person, and endured with a patience and fortitude that were Christ-like.'
>
> ('Reminiscences of Charlotte Brontë', *Scribner's Magazine*, 1871, Vol 2)

Surely Maria Brontë was the saddest of all that sad family. Of Miss Scatcherd, as Mrs Gaskell put it, Charlotte's:

'... heart, to the latest day on which we met, still beat with unavailing indignation at the worrying and the cruelty to which her gentle, patient, dying sister had been subjected by this woman.'

Thus that woman and her employer, Carus Wilson, went down to an unenviable posterity, deserving all the obloquy they brought upon their own heads.

Maria and then Elizabeth Brontë died. Charlotte at the age of eight found herself the eldest of the four children in her motherless family. She and Emily were brought back home by their father.

4. Growing Up

Charlotte and Emily joined Branwell and Anne at home with their father and Aunt Branwell. It was at this time that Tabitha Aykroyd arrived. Already a widow and fifty-four, she was to spend the next thirty years of her life until her death as beloved servant and family friend of the Brontë household. She provided the balance for the austere régime of Aunt Branwell. There is a little cameo that speaks volumes in the young Charlotte's 'History of the Year 1829':

> 'Tabby, the servant, is washing up the breakfast-things, and Anne, my youngest sister (Maria was my eldest), is kneeling on a chair, looking at some cakes which Tabby has been baking for us . . . Aunt is upstairs in her room, and I am sitting by the table writing this in the kitchen.'

In the late 1820s the writing careers of the Brontës began. Visiting Leeds in 1826, Mr Brontë came home with presents for the children which included a set of wooden soldiers for Branwell. Presented with these, Charlotte took one and exclaimed 'This is the Duke of Wellington! This shall be the Duke!' All the children chose, and around this set were built endless tales of war and battle enshrined in the so-called 'little writings', because they are minutely hand printed on tiny folded sheets of paper and stitched together into little books. Places and people were created, Great Glass Town came into being, later more sophisticatedly to become Verreopolis and Verdopolis. The Duke of Wellington gave way to an imaginary son, the Marquess of Douro. He had to have a land of his own, and so the kingdom of Angria was invented and Douro became Duke of Zamorna and King of Angria. Branwell conducted wars and revolutions, whilst Charlotte turned increasingly to the theme of love—Zamorna,

Patrick Brontë at the age of fifty-six. Ellen Nussey said 'Even at this time, Mr Brontë struck me as looking very venerable. . . . He was considered something of an invalid, and always lived in the most abstemious and simple manner.'

cruel, masterful and sexually irresistible. Meanwhile, Emily and Anne had created the Gondal saga which we know about only by report and ingeniously postulated reconstruction.

In 1831 the children were parted once again, and once more illness played a part. This time it was Mr Brontë's. He was struck down with congestion of the lungs and in his dangerous condition he realized that, were he to die, his children would not only be orphans but also homeless, unprovided for and incapable of making a living. Helped by her godparents, Thomas Atkinson (with whom Patrick had years before exchanged Hartshead for Thornton) and his wife, Charlotte was sent to another newly established school, Roe Head, run by Miss Margaret Wooler.

Roe Head was much nearer to Haworth than Cowan Bridge, only twenty miles away, and in the area where Patrick Brontë had served his first Yorkshire curacy, in the so-called Heavy Woollen district. To come here and to make friends with some who lived in this area was to give Charlotte first-hand knowledge of houses and locations which she would later combine with her father's historical recollections in writing *Shirley*.

Roe Head, despite its proximity to industrial areas, was also healthier than Cowan Bridge. Situated on the turnpike road from Leeds to Huddersfield about five miles from the latter place, it was a large, roomy Georgian house with three tiers of semicircular bow-windows looking down over its front lawns to Kirklees Park, on to the Calder valley in the middle distance and the hills around Huddersfield in the background. Mrs Gaskell writes:

> 'One of the bow-windowed rooms on the ground floor, with the pleasant look-out I have described, was the drawing-room; the other was the school-room. The dining-room was on one side of the door, and faced the road.'
>
> (*Life*, Chapter 6)

Inside, the house was oak panelled. Altogether it was a more imposing and more comfortable place than Cowan Bridge.

It differed in other respects also. Cowan Bridge looked to taking sixty or seventy pupils. Roe Head had a mere seven to ten. Above all, there was a difference in the atmosphere that proceeded from the difference in the character of the proprietor. The family were farmers with considerable property in the area and Margaret Wooler was the eldest of five sisters. Ellen Nussey remembers her thus:

> 'Personally, Miss Wooler was like a lady abbess. She wore white, well-fitting dresses embroidered. Her long hair plaited, formed a coronet, and long large ringlets fell from her head to shoulders. She was not pretty or handsome, but her quiet dignity made her presence imposing. She was nobly scrupulous and conscientious—a woman of the greatest self-denial.'
>
> (Quoted by C K Shorter, *The Brontës*: *Life and Letters*, 1908, Vol I, p 84)

But Charlotte was not happy at first. Ellen found her in the schoolroom— 'a silent, weeping, dark little figure in the large bay-window.' It was the beginning of a lasting friendship. Ellen was very prosaic but very loyal, a fine foil for the more passionate Charlotte. There were other friends, Mary Taylor of Gomersal and Martha, her sister, a boisterous dare-devil character, sadly, almost unbelievably for one of such vitality, to die at the early age of twenty-three—and worse, to die far from home and to be buried in a foreign grave. So much was Charlotte moved by this that she was to add a gratuitous paragraph to *Shirley*:

> 'But, Jessy, I will write about you no more. This is an autumn evening, wet and wild. There is only one cloud in the sky, but it

Margaret Wooler, a photograph taken in her later years (reproduced in *The Bookman*, October 1904). She ran her small school, Roe Head, conscientiously and instilled a love of learning in her pupils.

curtains it from pole to pole. The wind cannot rest; it hurries sobbing over hills of sullen outline, colourless with twilight and mist. Rain has beat all day on the church tower; it rises dark from the stony enclosure of its graveyard; the nettles, the long grass, and the tombs all drip with wet. This evening reminds me too forcibly of another evening some years ago—a howling, rainy autumn evening, too—when certain who had that day performed a pilgrimage to a grave new made in a heretic cemetery sat near a wood fire on the hearth of a foreign dwelling. They were merry and social, but they each knew that a gap, never to be filled, had been made in their circle. They knew they had lost something whose absence could never be quite atoned for so long as they lived; and they knew that heavy falling rain was soaking into the wet earth which covered their lost darling; and that the sad, sighing gale was mourning above her buried head. The fire warmed them; Life and Friendship yet blessed them; but Jessy lay cold, coffined, solitary—only the sod screening her from the storm.'

(*Shirley*, Chapter 23)

But that event lay in that future which from her experience of the past Charlotte Brontë seems always to have feared.

Roe Head, however, was to become an interval of happiness, a time for congenial study and the making of lasting friendships. How different from the Cowan Bridge régime was that which Mrs Gaskell described thus:

'When the girls were ready with their lessons, they came to Miss Wooler to say them. She had a remarkable knack of making them feel interested in whatever they had to learn. They set to their studies, not as to tasks or duties to be got through, but with a healthy desire and thirst for knowledge, of which she had managed to make them perceive the relishing savour. They did not leave off reading and learning as soon as the compulsory pressure of school was taken away. They had been taught to think, to analyze, to reject, to appreciate. Charlotte Brontë was happy in the choice made for her of the second school to which she was sent.'

(*Life*, Chapter 6)

But there was something better than Roe Head. That was the return home at the end of her schooldays, for Charlotte once again to be united with her family in the summer of 1832. The 'little writings' continued and, as she told Ellen:

'In the morning from nine o'clock till half past twelve, I instruct my sisters and draw, then we walk till dinner, after dinner I sew till tea time and after tea I either read, write, do a little fancy work or draw, as I please.'

[It should be noted that the Brontës followed the north country practice of midday dinner with tea time usually in the late afternoon or even early evening.]

Charlotte visited Ellen Nussey's home, Rydings, outside Birstall, for the first time in September 1832. She was accompanied by Branwell, then an impressionable fifteen year old. Ellen records his 'wild ecstasy with everything, ... taking views in every direction of the old turret-roofed house, the fine chestnut trees on the lawn ... and a large rookery.' Charlotte too, we are told, 'liked to pace the plantations or seek seclusion in the fruit garden.' Rydings, alas, is not now as then it was. The house remains, but the park and gardens are gone, sacrificed to roads and industry. Erskine Stuart, writing in 1888 when some but not all the damage had been done, records that:

Ellen Nussey as Charlotte drew her in the early years of their friendship. She lived
to be 80, dying in 1897.

'In former times, before the Leeds and Huddersfield road was cut
through the park, the Rydings was a beautiful residence, with
pleasant surroundings where grottoes, waterfalls, and fish ponds
were constructed, and in whose woods bluebells and starwort
wantoned in springtime in wild beauty.'

The change is the sadder because there are reasons for believing that
Rochester's home, Thornfield, in *Jane Eyre* may at least in part have been
modelled on Rydings. There Charlotte Brontë envisages a building:

' ... of proportions not vast, though considerable: a gentleman's
manor house, not a nobleman's seat: battlements round the top
gave it a picturesque look. Its grey front stood out well from the
background of a rookery, whose cawing tenants were now on the

View from Roe Head, still with factory chimneys, but fewer and the valley less smoke-ridden than in Charlotte's day. Down the valley was Rawfolds Mill, and some of the Luddites gathered in the field in front of the house prior to their attack on the Mill, although the Woolers were not there then.

Rydings, Birstall, home of
Charlotte's fellow pupil
and later lifelong friend,
Ellen Nussey. She must
have found the battlements,
trees and rookery appealing
and attractive.

Roe Head, Miss Wooler's school, some twenty miles from Haworth, where
Charlotte found some happiness after her previous experience of school at Cowan
Bridge. Here she worked very hard to make up for her patchy education, and was
noted for her short sightedness and Irish accent.

Opposite above
Summer: shadows on the moorland.
'A scene as fair and lone
As ever felt the soothing breeze'
Emily Brontë, 'The evening sun was sinking down'

Opposite below
The moors from Ponden Kirk, a panoramic view.
'Give we the hills our equal prayer,
Earth's breezy hills and heaven's blue sea;
I ask for nothing further here
But my own heart and liberty'
Emily Brontë, 'And like myself lone . . .'

Opposite
Top Withens, the isolated ruined farmhouse –
though occupied in the time of the Brontës –
and favoured identification of the fictional
Wuthering Heights.

Above right
The moors in spring.
'I would that in the withered grass
    Spring's budding wreaths we might discern,
The violet's eye might shyly flash,
    And young leaves shoot among the fern.'
Emily Brontë, 'How still, how happy . . .'

Below right
The Brontë Chair – the peculiar rock
formation which suggested the name.

wing: they flew over the lawn and grounds to alight in a great meadow, from which these were separated by a sunk fence, and where an array of mighty old thorn trees, strong, knotty, and broad as oaks, at once explained the etymology of the mansion's designation.'

(*Jane Eyre*, Chapter 11)

When Charlotte was at Rydings a terrible thunderstorm occurred, and that too may have provided material for the similar scene in *Jane Eyre* after Rochester's ill-fated proposal of marriage. The detail is accurate even to the lightning striking the chestnut tree:

'But what had befallen the night? The moon was not yet set, and we were all in shadow. I could scarcely see my master's face, near as I was. And what ailed the chestnut tree?—it writhed and groaned; while wind roared in the laurel walk, and came sweeping over us. . . . a livid, vivid spark leapt out of a cloud at which I was looking, and there was a crack, a crash, and a close rattling peal; . . . the great horse-chestnut at the bottom of the orchard had been struck by lightning in the night, and half of it split away. . . . [In the morning] Descending the laurel walk, I faced the wreck of the chestnut tree: it stood up black and riven; the trunk, split down the centre, gasped ghastly. The cloven halves were not broken from each other, for the firm base and strong roots kept them unsundered below; though community of vitality was destroyed—the sap could flow no more: their great boughs on each side were dead, and next winter's tempests would be sure to fell one or both to earth. As yet, however, they might be said to form one tree—a ruin, but an entire ruin.'

(*Jane Eyre*, Chapters 23, 25)

Ellen Nussey returned the visit in July 1833. Her reminiscences are especially helpful in giving an impression of the inhabitants of Haworth Parsonage. She notes Mr Brontë's venerable appearance, courteous manner and valetudinarian inclinations. She remarks also on Miss Branwell with her outmoded caps, 'front of light auburn curls', her dislike of the north and continuing nostalgia for Penzance. She remarks

Opposite above
Ponden Kirk, huge and ominous, model for Penistone Crag in *Wuthering Heights*.

Opposite below
Ponden Moor snow-covered.
'A cold white waste of snow-drifts lie'
Charlotte Brontë, 'Speak of the North'

too upon faithful, dependable Tabby Aykroyd, but it is what she has to say of the two younger Brontë sisters that is most interesting because it is one of the earliest impressions we have in any detail of Emily and Anne:

'Emily Brontë had by this time acquired a lithesome, graceful figure. She was the tallest person in the house, except her father. Her hair, which was naturally as beautiful as Charlotte's, was in the same unbecoming tight curl and frizz, and there was the same want of complexion. She had very beautiful eyes—kind, kindling, liquid eyes; but she did not often look at you; she was too reserved. . . . Their colour might be said to be dark grey, at other times dark blue, they varied so. She talked very little. She and Anne were like twins— inseparable companions, and in the very closest sympathy, which never had any interruption.

Anne—dear, gentle Anne—was quite different in appearance from the others. She was her aunt's favourite. Her hair was a very pretty, light brown, and fell on her neck in graceful curls. She had lovely violet-blue eyes, fine pencilled eyebrows, and clear, almost transparent complexion. She still pursued her studies, and especially her sewing, under the surveillance of her aunt. Emily had begun to have the disposal of her own time.'

This happy united household would not continue long.

5. Their Several Ways

On 2 July 1835 Charlotte wrote to Ellen Nussey:

> 'We are all about to divide, break up, separate . . . . I am sad—very sad—at the thought of leaving home; but duty—necessity—these are stern mistresses who will not be disobeyed.'

She was not half so sad as Emily. Both of them were to go to Roe Head, Emily as pupil and Charlotte returning as teacher. Branwell was to be sent to London, to the Royal Academy, to train for that artistic career to which he had neither the character to apply himself nor the talent to succeed. Ironically he had joined the Haworth Temperance Society at the end of 1834! He spent a week in London, probably drank his money away and returned to Haworth pretending he had been robbed. For better reasons Emily's absence was also of short duration. She returned, severely homesick, after about ten weeks. Charlotte remained with Miss Wooler till the spring of 1838, Anne having replaced Emily at the beginning of 1836. The school moved to Heald's House, Dewsbury Moor, in July 1837. Anne became ill; Miss Wooler in Charlotte's eyes paid not enough attention; Charlotte and probably her father, no doubt recollecting Cowan Bridge, Maria and Elizabeth, became fearful; the girls were called home. Meanwhile, Emily was enduring another of her brief absences, spending a short while as a teacher at Miss Patchett's Academy at Law Hill, Southowram, Halifax, before she too came back to Haworth at the end of March 1838.

From 1836 to 1838 Branwell was at home, becoming a freemason and indeed secretary of the local lodge, playing the church organ and, in the company of John Brown, the sexton, increasing his familiarity with the Black Bull. He was an entertaining conversationalist and a convivial, too

Stonegappe, Lothersdale
(near Skipton), where
Charlotte spent an unhappy
short spell as governess to
the Sidgwicks' five children
– 'I was never so glad to get
out of a house in my life'.

convivial, drinker. In May 1838, however, he set up as a portrait painter in Bradford—just when photography was the latest novelty! The venture lasted a year and he returned home.

The girls also had been at home, but in April 1839 Anne went as governess to the Inghams at Blake Hall, Mirfield, and a month later, Charlotte similarly to the Sidgwicks at Stonegappe, Lothersdale, near Skipton. This latter employment lasted little more than two months and by the end of the year Anne also was back home. The next move was Branwell's, to spend six months as tutor with the Postlethwaites at Broughton House, Broughton-in-Furness, in the course of which he did a painting of Broughton Church. He did others as well, painting when he should have been teaching. The result was dismissal yet again, though he persuaded his sisters that he had been unfairly rejected. He followed this job with eighteen months as a railway clerk at Sowerby Bridge and Luddendenfoot before being dismissed for alleged default in the accounts. Charlotte made one more attempt at governessing in March 1841, this time with the Whites at Upperwood House, Rawdon near Leeds. A year previously Anne had gone to the Robinsons at Thorp Green, Little Ouseburn near York where Branwell was to join her at the beginning of 1843 and whence both were to leave in the summer of 1845.

Emily's sojourn at Law Hill was disastrous; 'slavery' Charlotte called it, in a large school of forty pupils, working from six in the morning to eleven at night. Charlotte had her sympathies and worries for Anne too, as she wrote to Ellen Nussey:

> 'She has so much to endure. When my thoughts turn to her, they always see her as a patient, persecuted stranger .... She is more lonely, less gifted with the power of making friends, even than I am.'
>
> (7 August 1841)

Some of this feeling may have arisen from Charlotte's own extreme distaste for work which her proud spirit resented. Even of the Roe Head experience she had asked: 'Am I forced to spend all the best part of my life in this wretched bondage?' At Stonegappe she found Mrs Sidgwick overbearing and unsympathetic and the children 'little devils incarnate', though there is other testimony that says that she herself by her proud and independent spirit did little to endear herself to the family. Charlotte found Mrs Sidgwick devoid 'of every fine feeling, of every gentle and delicate sentiment.' (1 July 1839) Mrs White also (as to some extent her

Opposite
Law Hill, Southowram, scene of Emily's brief unhappy spell as a teacher. It was built in 1771 and became a school in 1825.

husband, though Charlotte thought better of the men than of the women) was judged and found wanting for her vulgarity, coarse unladylike passions and bad grammar! A visitor to the Whites remembered Charlotte as 'a shy nervous girl, ill at ease, who desired to escape notice and to avoid taking part in the general conversation.' (C K Shorter, *The Brontës: Life and Letters*, 1908, Vol I, p 203).

During her brief stay with the Sidgwicks Charlotte may have visited Swarcliffe near Harrogate. According to Ellen Nussey, she went with them to the three-storeyed fourteenth-century manor house at Norton Conyers and to nearby Wath Church, though both this visit and the stay at Swarcliffe itself are questioned by many Brontë scholars. The house answers to some of the particulars of Thornfield in *Jane Eyre*, among them the story of the madwoman confined there in an upper room, the attic rooms full of old furniture, the oak-panelled staircase and hall with its coats of armour, the two-leaved door of the dining-room, even the rookery and gardens which were more extensive than those of the other claimant, Rydings. In the novel we read:

> 'Traversing the long and matted gallery, I descended the slippery steps of oak; then I gained the hall. I halted there a minute; I looked at some pictures on the walls (one, I remember, represented a grim man in a cuirass, and one a lady with powdered hair and a pearl necklace), at a bronze lamp pendent from the ceiling, at a great clock whose case was of oak curiously carved, and ebon black with time and rubbing. Everything appeared very stately and imposing to me; but then I was so little accustomed to grandeur. The hall door, which was half of glass, stood open; I stepped over the threshold. It was a fine autumn morning; the early sun shone serenely on embrowned groves and still green fields. Advancing on to the lawn, I looked up and surveyed the front of the mansion. It was three stories high, of proportions not vast, though considerable: a gentleman's manor house, not a nobleman's seat: battlements round the top gave it a picturesque look. Its grey front stood out well from the background of a rookery, whose cawing tenants were now on the wing: they flew over the lawn and grounds to alight in a great meadow, from which these were separated by a sunk fence, and where an array of mighty old thorn trees, strong, knotty, and broad as oaks, at once explained the etymology of the mansion's

Opposite
Norton Conyers, sometimes but doubtfully claimed as a model for Thornfield in *Jane Eyre*, where Charlotte may have visited with the Sidgwicks during their stay with the Greenwoods at Swarcliffe near Harrogate.

designation.... The large front chambers I thought especially grand; and some of the third-story rooms, though dark and low, were interesting from their air of antiquity. The furniture once appropriated to the lower apartments had from time to time been removed here, as fashions changed, and the imperfect light entering by their narrow casements showed bedsteads of a hundred years old; chests in oak or walnut, looking, with their strange carvings of palm branches and cherubs' heads, like types of the Hebrew ark; rows of venerable chairs, high-backed and narrow; stools still more

antiquated, on whose cushioned tops were yet apparent traces of half-effaced embroideries, wrought by fingers that for two generations had been coffin-dust.'

(*Jane Eyre*, Chapter 11)

Norton Conyers makes some claims by virtue of its rookery and of its madwoman's attic. As we have noted, however, there was also a rookery at Rydings and there may have been attic quarters for the insane as well. There was madness in the Nussey family itself. There is the problem of 'the church at the gates'. As Jane gazes down from the battlement, she sees:

' ... the grounds laid out like a map; the bright and velvet lawn closely girdling the grey base of the mansion; the field, wide as a park, dotted with its ancient timber; the wood, dun and sere, divided by a path visibly overgrown, greener with moss than the trees were with foliage; the church at the gates, the road, the tranquil hills, all reposing in the autumn day's sun.'

(*Jane Eyre*, Chapter 11)

To see Wath Church Charlotte would have had to look from the back of Norton Conyers, and, even so, it is hardly so near as to be described as being 'at the gates'.

What other argument may be adduced? On the occasion of the ill-fated attempted marriage-ceremony in the novel we are told that the strangers stood in:

'... that quiet and humble temple ... by the vault of the Rochesters, ... viewing through the rails the old time-stained marble tomb where a kneeling angel guarded the remains of Damer de Rochester, slain at Marston Moor in the time of the Civil Wars, and of Elizabeth, his wife.'

(*Jane Eyre*, Chapter 28)

Could this church have been Wath? Erskine Stuart made comparison with Sir Richard Graham, first baronet of Norton Conyers, but there is no tomb in Wath Church to this man and, though several 'sepulchral monuments' are said to have been removed in the course of the vandalism that went under the name of restoration in the 1870s, no such tomb could have been there since Sir Richard was not killed at Marston Moor but died peacefully in his bed a decade later. Moreover, the Grahams have their own chapel in the south transept of Wath Church, so there was little likelihood of a tomb behind the rails. A novelist, of course, has licence to

The ruins at Wycoller showing the old fireplace where 'his head supported against the high, old-fashioned mantelpiece, appeared the blind tenant of the room [Rochester].' (*Jane Eyre*, Chapter 37)

adapt, and it is perhaps just possible that in this particular Charlotte Brontë may have gained her seminal idea from visiting Norton Conyers, if she ever went there. Sir Richard's portrait with the record of his turning out at Marston Moor is to be found in the oak-panelled hall on the very wall on which the pieces of armour are displayed.

There is another house in *Jane Eyre*—Ferndean, to which Rochester retreated after Thornfield was destroyed by fire. There he lived maimed and blind and thither Jane was called by telepathy, parapsychology or call it what you will. Charlotte Brontë describes Jane's approach:

'Even when within a very short distance of the manor house you could see nothing of it, so thick and dark grew the timber of the

The packhorse bridge
at Wycoller.

gloomy wood about it. Iron gates between granite pillars showed me where to enter, and passing through them, I found myself at once in the twilight of close-ranked trees. There was a grass-grown track descending the forest aisle between hoar and knotty shafts and under branched arches. I followed it, expecting soon to reach the dwelling; but it stretched on and on, it wound far and farther: no sign of habitation or grounds was visible . . . . I proceeded. At last my way opened, the trees thinned a little; presently I beheld a railing, then the house—scarce, by this dim light, distinguishable from the trees, so dank and green were its decaying walls. Entering a portal, fastened only by a latch, I stood amidst a space of enclosed ground, from which the wood swept away in a semicircle. There were no flowers, no garden-beds; only a broad gravel-walk girdling a grass-plat, and this set in the heavy frame of the forest. The house presented two pointed gables in its front; the windows were latticed and narrow: the front door was narrow too, one step led up to it. The whole looked, as the host of the Rochester Arms had said, "quite a desolate spot".'

(*Jane Eyre*, Chapter 37)

There is little there about the house itself, though earlier she had called it 'a building of considerable antiquity, moderate size, and no architectural pretensions', and later in the highly dramatic scene of Jane's and Rochester's reconciliation we are told that:

'This parlour looked gloomy. A neglected handful of fire burnt in the grate; and leaning over it with his head supported against the high, old-fashioned mantelpiece, appeared the blind tenant of the room.'

(*Jane Eyre*, Chapter 37)

It is perhaps this last detail of its construction that has led to the widespread equation of Ferndean with the ruins of Wycoller Hall, notable for its great round circular stone fireplace and situation some eight miles from Haworth over the Lancashire border towards Colne. It should be added that another claimant for the Ferndean identification is Kirklees Hall, which also figures in *Shirley* as Nunnwood.

Life as governess in these years in which they went their several ways did nothing to repress the sisters' continuing literary activity, even though by its demands and by their separation it placed severe restrictions upon it. Charlotte, in fact, severed herself from the Angrian writings in 1839, but Emily, more at home than the rest, continued to pour forth poetry and prose for the Gondal series. It should be pointed

Easton Farm, Bridlington: the water-colour Charlotte painted while staying there
in 1839 with Ellen Nussey.

out that the common idea of the Brontë sisters as secluded, untutored and
unread geniuses cannot stand up to scrutiny. One need go no further than
Charlotte's letter of 4 July 1834 to Ellen Nussey which sets out a veritable
reading course in classical English texts—fiction, biography, poetry and
history—from Shakespeare to such contemporaries as Southey and
Wordsworth. These two names remind us of other activity in these years,
the attempts especially by Branwell but also by Charlotte to interest and
enlist the help of the influential for their literary efforts. Branwell's
badgering of *Blackwood's Magazine* and his arrogant approach to
Wordsworth met blank silence, but he succeeded better, and probably
not to his good, with a letter of encouragement from Hartley Coleridge.
Employing greater tact, Charlotte received a better response, even if
sobering and not very encouraging, from Wordsworth and Southey.

   After quitting the service of the Sidgwicks Charlotte paid a visit in
September 1839 with Ellen Nussey to Burlington (Bridlington). There she
gained her first sight of the sea, an experience that filled her with such
concurrent pain and pleasure that she wept on both accounts. They
stayed first with the Hudsons at Easton, about two miles from the coast,

and Charlotte painted a water-colour of their farmhouse, but for the final week of the three-week visit they moved into lodgings on Bridlington Quay, there to enjoy uninterrupted proximity to the ocean.

It was in the middle of the 1830s that Patrick Brontë obtained the first in his succession of curates. He was William Hodgson, to be followed by lovely and beloved Willie Weightman, attractive to the girls of the whole neighbourhood but to meet an early death and to be most lamented by Anne who in her quiet way had fallen deeply in love with him. It may well be that she fantasized the might-have-been in *Agnes Grey* as the heroine thinks of her curate:

> 'To be near him, to hear him talk as he did talk; and to feel that he thought me worthy to be so spoken to—capable of understanding and duly appreciating such discourse—was enough. Yes, Edward Weston, I could indeed be happy in a house full of enemies, if I had but one friend, who truly, deeply, and faithfully loved me; and if that friend were you—though we might be far apart—. . . it would be too much happiness to dream of!'
>
> (*Agnes Grey*, Chapter 20)

That sounds much as Anne might have felt as governess near York, thinking of Willie Weightman at Haworth. And surely also it was of him she wrote:

> 'Yes, thou art gone! and never more
> Thy sunny smile shall gladden me. . . .
> The lightest heart that I have known,
> The kindest I shall ever know.'

The years with the Robinsons at Little Ouseburn gave Anne important material for both her novels. Charlotte has Jane Eyre act as a governess but it is in an unusual situation of looking after one child, and that the extraordinary ward of Rochester with all the strange circumstances of Celine Varens' background. In fact, Charlotte probably drew most closely on her experience as governess in the first part of *Jane Eyre* where she portrays the cruelty and oppression exerted by the Reed children on the orphan Jane.

Their behaviour has plentiful parallel in the experiences of Agnes

Opposite
Different moorland: the scenery of the Peak District, close to which Charlotte stayed on her visit to Hathersage, only four and a half miles from Eyam, the famous Plague Village, and a good centre for exploring the lovely Peak District.

The northern part of the Peak District is heather-clad gritstone, and less populated than Charlotte Brontë's familiar moors. The highest peak is Kinder Scout, at 2000 feet, actually part of a vast plateau, and north west of Hathersage.

Grey in her first post in the Bloomfield household. Bloomfield himself, it is hinted, is underbred. Like Rochester, he meets his governess first in a situation where neither has been properly introduced to the other. In this instance, however, the governess is not struck by the master's manner or appearance. He chides her for not controlling his disobedient children. Agnes's comment, which serves by simple statement to place his behaviour, is:

> '"I was surprised that he should nominate his children Master and Miss Bloomfield [*there is the upstart!*]; and still more so, that he should speak so uncivilly to me, their governess, and a perfect stranger to himself."'
>
> (*Agnes Grey*, Chapter 3)

Unable to bribe and forbidden to punish, Agnes can make little impression upon her recalcitrant charges. The boy Tom exults in cruelty to animals, proposing, for instance, to roast a bird alive. He even assaults his governess. Anne Brontë, probably transcribing her own experience, tells of Agnes sitting in front of Tom imprisoned in a corner 'twisting his body and face into the most grotesque and singular contortions . . . and uttering loud yells and doleful outcries.' Mary Ann, however, is even

Opposite above
View of Haworth, with typical nineteenth-century
mill, from Braemoor.

Opposite below
Cows graze peacefully; rural scene from the churchyard at Hathersage.

Easton Farm, Bridlington, today, the long low farmhouse which belonged to the
Hudsons, friends of Ellen Nussey, where she and Charlotte stayed in August
1839.

worse, throwing herself on the ground and presenting a dead weight when any attempt is made to lift her up:

> 'In vain I argued, coaxed, entreated, threatened, scolded; in vain I kept her in from play, or, if obliged to take her out, refused to play with her, or to speak kindly, or have anything to do with her.'
> (Agnes Grey, Chapter 3)

Nor can Agnes do anything to satisfy Mr Bloomfield:

> 'If I were quiet at the moment, I was conniving at their disorderly conduct; if (as was frequently the case) I happened to be exalting my voice to enforce order, I was using undue violence, and setting the girls a bad example by such ungentleness of tone and language.'
> (Agnes Grey, Chapter 4)

Agnes determines that in such a situation 'Patience, Firmness, and Perseverance, were [her] only weapons; and these [she] resolved to use to the utmost.' (Chapter 3) Not with very satisfactory results, or even perhaps with the chance of such.

It might be that the Bloomfields are some kind of transcript of Anne's experiences with the Inghams at Mirfield. Certainly for her next post Agnes travels, as did Anne to the Robinsons at Little Ouseburn, some seventy miles from home, and one wonders whether Horton Lodge, the residence of the Murrays, in some ways replicated Thorp Green (which has now disappeared). Anne tells us of this 'very respectable' house with 'a wide park, stocked with deer, and beautified by fine old trees'. Surely she speaks of the contrast with home when she goes on:

> 'The surrounding country itself was pleasant, as far as fertile fields, flourishing trees, quiet green lanes, and smiling hedges with wild flowers scattered along their banks could make it; but it was depressingly flat to one born and nurtured among the rugged hills of———.'
> (Agnes Grey, Chapter 7)

It is a more subtle form of oppression that Agnes undergoes at Horton Lodge. Mrs Murray speaks from a different level of social status than that of the Bloomfields. She has different expectations for her children. Of these, the eldest, Rosalie, is bent only on 'coming out', conscious of her position, at first overbearing, then merely patronizing to the governess:

'She had never been perfectly taught the distinction between right and wrong; she had, like her brothers and sisters been suffered, from infancy, to tyrannize over nurses, governesses, and servants; she had not been taught to moderate her desires, to control her temper or bridle her will, or to sacrifice her own pleasure for the good of others.'

(*Agnes Grey*, Chapter 7)

So far as education is concerned, she is interested only in such social accomplishments as singing, dancing, drawing, and French and German. Of the other children Matilda is a hoyden interested mainly in horses; John is 'a young bear, boisterous, unruly, unprincipled, untaught, unteachable', and Charles is 'a pettish, cowardly, capricious, selfish little fellow, only active in doing mischief and only clever in inventing falsehoods.'

The latter part of *Agnes Grey* is, in fact, devoted mainly to Rosalie's entry into the world and, in lesser degree, to Agnes's love for the curate, Weston. There are still, however, passages that show the sufferings and persecutions endured by the governess—not only rebuke but patronage with it, as in Mrs Murray's lecture to Agnes about her failure with Matilda:

'"The young lady's proficiency and elegance is of more consequence to the governess than her own, as well as to the world. If she wishes to prosper in her vocation she must devote all her energies to her business: all her ideas and all her ambition will tend to the accomplishment of that one object. When we wish to decide upon the merits of a governess, we naturally look at the young ladies she professes to have educated, and judge accordingly. The *judicious* governess knows this: she knows that, while she lives in obscurity herself, her pupil's virtues and defects will be open to every eye; and that, unless she loses sight of herself in their cultivation, she need not hope for success. You see, Miss Grey, it is just the same as any other trade or profession: they that wish to prosper must devote themselves body and soul to their calling; and if they begin to yield to indolence or self-indulgence they are speedily distanced by wiser competitors: there is little to choose between a person that ruins her pupils by neglect, and one that corrupts them by her example. You will excuse my dropping these little hints: you know it is all for your own good. Many ladies would speak to you much more strongly; and many would not trouble themselves to speak at all, but quietly look out for a substitute. That, of course, would be the *easiest* plan: but I know the advantages of a place like this to a person in your situation; and I have no desire to part with you, as I am sure you would do very well if you will only think of these things and try to exert yourself a *little* more: then, I am convinced, you would *soon* acquire that delicate tact which alone is wanting to give you a proper influence over the mind of your pupil."

I was about to give the lady some idea of the fallacy of her expectations; but she sailed away as soon as she had concluded her speech. Having said what she wished, it was no part of her plan to await my answer: it was my business to hear, and not to speak.'

(*Agnes Grey*, Chapter 18)

The sojourn at Little Ouseburn also gave Anne the unwanted but inescapable chance of watching Branwell in his drinking habits, an experience which enabled her, to the disgust of some of her more easily offended Victorian readers, to portray the alcoholic decline of Arthur Huntingdon in *The Tenant of Wildfell Hall*. Indeed, one wonders whether the references to Lady Lowborough's 'criminal connections with Mr Huntingdon' in that novel may spring from things that Anne knew about Branwell's relations with Mrs Robinson. It is, however, the analysis of the circumstances of alcoholic addiction which commands most attention. Little is made of the physical effects, much of the psychological. After the marriage Helen Huntingdon notes her husband's boredom, his inability to interest himself in anything:

'If he would play the country gentleman, and attend to the farm — but that he knows nothing about, and won't give his mind to consider — or if he would take up with some literary study, or learn to draw or to play . . . but he is far too idle for such an undertaking.'

(*The Tenant of Wildfell Hall*, Chapter 25)

London in the season and the grouse moors in theirs are his only occupations. Anne Brontë traces the increasing dependence on the 'stimulus of wine . . . now something more to him than an accessory to social enjoyment; it was an important source of enjoyment in itself.' (Chapter 30) Huntingdon becomes irritable and irrational; he rejects the kindly approaches of his wife and in his illness considers her ministry only as a means by which she may gain revenge upon him. He waves aside Helen's remonstrances about his continued drinking. Throwing the bottle of diluted port through the window and calling for the strongest wine, he 'seized a glass in one hand and the bottle in the other, and never rested till he had drunk it dry.' (Chapter 49) The novel moves remorselessly to the hopeless death bed scene, to the death itself and the one brief reference to Huntingdon's physical condition, and that only to his corpse: 'His body will be consigned on Thursday to that dark grave he so much dreaded; but the coffin must be closed as soon as possible.' (Chapter 49) The history of Henry Huntingdon does not, even for our more robust generation, make pleasant reading, but none can deny that it is accurately observed. That was what Anne had to regard in Branwell.

6. Those 'Wuthering' Heights

If any of the Brontë novels is quintessential, it must be *Wuthering Heights*, for it is in that book that we get the real sense of the moors. The very title—with its northernism 'a significant provincial adjective', in the narrator Lockwood's words '... descriptive of the atmospheric tumult to which [the house by] its station is exposed in stormy weather' (Chapter 1)—directs us compellingly to the harshness of the place. The novel itself portrays a confined world of fierce passions—jealousy, hatred, and love as hard as hatred. Consider only the elder Cathy's dying declaration to Heathcliff in which her ferocity and bitterness towards the man she loves, and cannot help herself from loving, from the depths of her heart, drives her to wish him suffering in an embrace from which neither would emerge alive. It is terrifying, and from what we know of Emily Brontë she was capable of behaviour no less overpowering, no less terrifying. There is the famous story of her beating the disobedient dog, Keeper:

> 'Her bare clenched fist struck against his fierce red eyes, before he had time to make his spring, and, in the language of the turf, she "punished him" till his eyes swelled up and the half-blind, stupefied beast was led to his accustomed lair, to have his swollen head fomented and cared for by the very Emily herself.'
>
> (*Life*, Chapter 12)

There was an affinity between the woman and her environment, the passionate human being and the wild surroundings, such that, as we have seen, she became physically ill when she was separated from it. As Charlotte put it in the Preface to the 1850 edition of *Wuthering Heights*:

'Ellis Bell did not describe as one whose eye and taste alone found pleasure in the prospect; her native hills were far more to her than a spectacle; they were what she lived in, and by, as much as the wild birds, their tenants, or as the heather, their produce.'

That was why on that first departure to Miss Wooler's school in 1835 she had so quickly to return. As Charlotte reports:

'My sister Emily loved the moors. Flowers brighter than the rose bloomed in the blackest of the heath for her; out of a sudden hollow in a livid hillside, her mind could make an Eden. She found in the bleak solitude many and dear delights; and not the least and best-loved was—liberty. Liberty was the breath of Emily's nostrils; without it she perished.'

(*Life*, Chapter 8)

That was why with the sisters together again the spring of 1844 was such a marvellous delight: 'The moors were a great resource this spring; Emily and Charlotte walked out on them perpetually.' (*Life*, Chapter 13) Even dear prosaic Ellen Nussey appreciated Emily's special affection for the moors:

'One long ramble made in these early days was far away over the moors to a spot familiar to Emily and Anne, which they called "The Meeting of the Waters". It was a small oasis of emerald green turf, broken here and there by small clear springs; a few large stones served as resting-places; seated here, we were hidden from all the world, nothing appearing in view but miles and miles of heather, a glorious blue sky, and brightening sun.'
('Reminiscences of Charlotte Brontë', *Scribner's Magazine*, 1871, Vol 2)

Charlotte testified in a letter to James Taylor (of Smith, Elder) (22 May 1850) that 'there is not a knoll of heather, not a branch of fern, not a young bilberry leaf, not a fluttering lark or linnet, but reminds me of her.' In *Wuthering Heights* Emily celebrates the moors in every season and every type of weather. Passage after passage testifies to closest observation of their ever-changing but always loved appearance. When after Heathcliff's death Lockwood makes a short summer visit to the area of his former residence, Emily records the two extreme opposites of the face of the land:

The Brontë Bridge over Sladen Beck. Nearby is the Brontë Chair. 'A few large stones served as resting places. . . . Emily, half reclined on a slab of stone, played like a young child with the tadpoles in the water.'—Ellen Nussey on her visit in 1833.

'It was sweet, warm weather—too warm for travelling; but the heat did not hinder me from enjoying the delightful scenery above and below; had I seen it nearer August, I'm sure it would have tempted me to waste a month among its solitudes. In winter, nothing more dreary, in summer, nothing more divine, than those glens shut in by hills, and those bluff, bold swells of heath.'

(*Wuthering Heights*, Chapter 32)

Despite Lockwood, winter is the time to see the moors. They are glorious in summer, especially in late summer, with their rich spreading purple heather carpet, but nothing surpasses them when the blackened soil, the deep grey boulders, the dying heather and the browning bracken are lightly covered with the early snows of winter and the bilberry and crowberry manage still to show green amid the otherwise desolate landscape. Cathy was buried during a snowfall and Heathcliff went alone to her grave, mad to embrace her one last time, cold on the moors as the sleet-laden wind swept over them. (*Wuthering Heights*, Chapter 29)

From the experience of weather like that the coming spring in early March is all the more joyfully welcomed. There is a touching scene as Edgar Linton brings the dying Cathy the first evidence of new life which spring has produced. He brings crocuses:

'Her eye, long stranger to any gleam of pleasure, caught them in waking, and shone delighted as she gathered them eagerly together.

"These are the earliest flowers at the Heights!" she exclaimed. "They remind me of soft thaw winds, and warm sunshine, and nearly melted snow. Edgar, is there not a south wind, and is not the snow almost gone?"

"The snow is quite gone down here, darling," replied her husband; "and I only see two white spots on the whole range of moors—the sky is blue, and the larks are singing, and the becks and brooks are all brim full. Catherine, last spring at this time, I was longing to have you under this roof—now, I wish you were a mile or two up those hills; the air blows so sweetly, I feel that it would cure you."

"I shall never be there, but once more!" said the invalid; "and then you'll leave me, and I shall remain, for ever."'

(*Wuthering Heights*, Chapter 13)

Emily describes the moors not only in the differing seasons, but also under every variation of weather. There is the long line of September mist seen by Edgar and Cathy as they gaze up the Gimmerton valley, 'Wuthering Heights rose above this silvery vapour.' (Chapter 10) There is the thunderous evening when Nelly Dean meets the shepherd-boy frightened by seeing the ghosts of 'Heathcliff and a woman yonder, under t'Nab'. (Chapter 34) There are Nelly Dean and the younger Cathy:

> 'On an afternoon in October, or the beginning of November, a fresh watery afternoon, when the turf and paths were rustling with moist, withered leaves, and the cold, blue sky was half-hidden by clouds, dark grey streamers, rapidly mounting from the west and boding abundant rain . . .'
>
> (*Wuthering Heights*, Chapter 22)

The spreading sky and the scurrying clouds, on the one hand; the last lone flower on the other:

> '"Look, Miss!" I exclaimed, pointing to a nook under the roots of one twisted tree. "Winter is not here yet. There's a little flower, up yonder, the last bud from the multitude of bluebells that clouded those turf steps in July with a lilac mist. Will you clamber up, and pluck it to show to papa?"
>
> Cathy stared a long time at the lonely blossom trembling in its earthly shelter, and replied, at length—
>
> "No, I'll not touch it—but it looks melancholy, does it not, Ellen?" . . .
>
> "No," she repeated, and continued sauntering on, pausing, at intervals, to muse over a bit of moss, or a tuft of blanched grass, or a fungus spreading its bright orange among the heaps of brown foliage.'
>
> (*Wuthering Heights*, Chapter 22)

If that is late autumn, there are the two visions of bright July. The younger Cathy is contrasting her idea with that of Linton Heathcliff:

> 'He said the pleasantest manner of spending a hot July day was lying from morning till evening on a bank of heath in the middle of the moors, with the bees humming dreamily about among the bloom, and the larks singing high up overhead, and the blue sky and bright sun shining steadily and cloudlessly. That was his most perfect idea of heaven's happiness—mine was rocking in a rustling green tree, with a west wind blowing, and bright, white clouds flitting rapidly above; and not only larks, but throstles, and blackbirds, and linnets, and cuckoos pouring out music on every side, and the moors seen at a distance, broken into cool dusky dells; but close by great swells of long grass undulating in waves to the breeze; and woods and

Shibden Hall, near Halifax, can be seen across the valley from Law Hill and is
suggested by some to be the model for Thrushcross Grange.

sounding water, and the whole world awake and wild with joy. He
wanted all to lie in an ecstasy of peace; I wanted all to sparkle, and
dance in a glorious jubilee.'

(Wuthering Heights, Chapter 24)

The younger Cathy possessed her mother's adventurous spirit, and
confinement to Thrushcross Grange restricted her desire for broader
horizons:

"'Ellen, how long will it be before I can walk to the top of those
hills? I wonder what lies on the other side—is it the sea?'

"No, Miss Cathy," I would answer, "it is hills again just like
these."

"And what are those golden rocks like, when you stand under
them?" she once asked.

The abrupt descent of Penistone Crags particularly attracted her
notice, especially when the setting sun shone on it, and the topmost
heights; and the whole extent of landscape besides lay in shadow.

View across the moor.
'In all the lonely landscape round
I see no light and hear no sound
Except the wind that far away
Comes sighing o'er the heathy sea'
Emily Brontë, 'The sun has set'

Ponden Hall, below Stanbury, on the way to Wycoller, in the valley (with Top Withens on the heights), the favoured location of Thrushcross Grange.

I explained that they were bare masses of stone, with hardly enough earth in their clefts to nourish a stunted tree.

"And why are they bright so long after it is evening here?" she pursued.

"Because they are a great deal higher up than we are," replied I; "you could not climb them, they are too high and steep. In winter the frost is always there before it comes to us; and deep into summer, I have found snow under that black hollow on the north-east side!"'

(*Wuthering Heights*, Chapter 18)

In vain Nelly Dean attempts to persuade her that 'Thrushcross Park is the finest place in the world.' Wuthering Heights and Thrushcross Grange form a structural contrast within the novel. The Grange is sheltered in the valley. It is a place of comfort:

' . . . a splendid place carpeted with crimson, and crimson-covered chairs and tables, and a pure white ceiling bordered by gold, a shower of glass drops hanging in silver chains from the centre, and shimmering with little soft tapers.'

(*Wuthering Heights*, Chapter 6)

So Heathcliff and Cathy note as they gaze through the windows. Inside the Linton children quarrel over a pet dog: it is a place of luxury, but it is also effete.

There are rival candidates for the possible identification of Wuthering Heights and Thrushcross Grange among real houses. Phyllis Bentley, that Brontë devotee and not inconsiderable novelist herself, feels that Emily's stay at Law Hill School may have led to two old houses in that district being in her mind as likely equivalents—Shibden Hall lying in the valley and looking across to High Sunderland on the hill. It is more usual, however, to identify Thrushcross with Ponden Hall, near Stanbury, the home of the Heaton family, and Top (or High) Withens on the moors above Haworth as the equivalent of Wuthering Heights.

Top Withens, desolate and now in ruins, exposed to all that wind and weather may bring down, stands lonely amidst the wild, rolling moors, an appropriate home for those passionate spirits who belong to Wuthering Heights. The Heights are exposed:

'"Wuthering" being a significant provincial adjective, descriptive of the atmospheric tumult to which its station is exposed in stormy weather. Pure, bracing ventilation they must have up there at all times, indeed: one may guess the power of the north wind, blowing over the edge, by the excessive slant of a few stunted firs at the end of the house; and by a range of gaunt thorns all stretching their limbs one way, as if craving alms of the sun. Happily, the architect had foresight to build it strong: the narrow windows are deeply set in the wall, and the corners defended with large jutting stones.'

(*Wuthering Heights*, Chapter 1)

As Lockwood, the narrator of the story, describes the house:

'The family sitting-room [was] without any introductory lobby or passage: they call it here "the house" pre-eminently. It includes kitchen, and parlour, generally, but I believe at Wuthering Heights the kitchen is forced to retreat altogether into another quarter, at least I distinguished a chatter of tongues, and a clatter of culinary utensils, deep within; and I observed no signs of roasting, boiling, or baking, about the huge fireplace; nor any glitter of copper saucepans and tin cullenders on the walls. One end, indeed, reflected splendidly both light and heat, from ranks of immense pewter dishes, interspersed with silver jugs and tankards, towering row after row, in a vast oak dresser, to the very roof. The latter had never been underdrawn, its entire anatomy laid bare to an inquiring eye, except where a frame of wood laden with oatcakes, and clusters of legs of beef, mutton, and ham, concealed it. Above the chimney were sundry villainous old guns, and a couple of horse-pistols, and, by way of ornament, three gaudily painted canisters disposed along its ledge. The floor was of smooth, white stone: the chairs, high-backed, primitive structures, painted green: one or two heavy black ones lurking in the shade. In an arch, under the dresser, reposed a huge, liver-coloured bitch pointer surrounded by a swarm of squealing puppies; and other dogs haunted other recesses.'

(*Wuthering Heights*, Chapter 1)

That was the first visit. When Lockwood ventured on a second occasion 'on that bleak hilltop the earth was hard with a bleak frost and the air made [him] shiver through every limb'. (Chapter 2) That was the wind and weather, but there was more to the occasion than that. Reaching the gate, ' . . . being unable to remove the chain, [he] jumped over, and, . . . knocked vainly for admittance till [his] knuckles tingled, and the dogs howled.' Joseph, the 'vinegar-faced' old servant, eventually opened an upstairs window and spoke to him, but would not let him in. Entrance was only secured when he was led round by the back way. It was a difficult approach to be followed by an unfriendly welcome. Heathcliff's first words were to dispel any illusion that Lockwood might have about getting back home in the snowstorm either soon or alone. Amidst the evident savagery of the domestic atmosphere of Wuthering Heights Lockwood made things worse by stumbling from one *faux pas* to another as he conjectures the relationships of the several characters in the household. Surly faces, sharp utterances and, in the case of Heathcliff, contemptuous dismissals of Lockwood's errors set the tone for the reader's introduction to this terrifying abode.

The weather, the moors, this house provide the setting for the unique and amazing story that issued from Emily Brontë's overpowering

Opposite above
Birstall Church, model for Briarfield, in the churchyard of which Shirley and Caroline hid during the attack on Moore's mill.

Opposite below
Non-conformist chapel near Red House, Gomersal, house of the Taylor family the Yorkes of *Shirley* and there called Briarmains.

Oakwell Hall, Fieldhead of *Shirley*. Built in 1583, a semi-fortified Elizabethan manor house. It includes some ancient timbers from an earlier building, and is now a museum.

Opposite above
Kirklees Park with the Hall in the background, Nunnely Park and Nunnwood in *Shirley*. A small Cistercian Nunnery stood there once, possibly the nunnery where Robin Hood died; it was closed during the Dissolution.

Opposite below
Oakwell Hall – the great hall with large open fireplace and balcony.

imagination, a story of high passions and suffering, of sadistic persecution, of love and cruelty and of the two fused together in the terrible
oneness of the elder Cathy's and Heathcliff's irresistible attraction to
each other. After making the mistake of being seduced by the seemingly
superior but really superficial appearances of Thrushcross and choosing
therefore to marry Edgar Linton in the years when Heathcliff had been
terrorized and barbarized by Hindley Earnshaw, the elder Cathy quickly
realizes her mistake. Edgar, quiet, civilized, balanced, but essentially
passionless, is no proper match for this headstrong girl who in any case
has her inescapable 'soul-mate' relationship with Heathcliff, the mysteri-
ous waif whom her father had one day brought home with him to become
the favoured inmate and thus to make Hindley, the Earnshaw son,
jealous beyond enduring.

Cathy and Heathcliff belong in spirit to each other. In a famous
passage she declares:

> '"My great miseries in this world have been Heathcliff's miseries,
> and I watched and felt each from the beginning; my great thought in
> living is himself. If all else perished, and *he* remained, I should still
> continue to be; and if all else remained, and he were annihilated, the
> universe would turn to a mighty stranger. I should not seem a part of
> it. My love for Linton is like the foliage in the woods. Time will
> change it, I'm well aware, as winter changes the trees. My love for
> Heathcliff resembles the eternal rocks beneath—a source of little
> visible delight, but necessary. Nelly, I *am* Heathcliff—he's always,
> always in my mind—not as a pleasure, any more than I am always a
> pleasure to myself—but as my own being."'
>
> (*Wuthering Heights*, Chapter 9)

After the encounter between Linton and Heathcliff and as her husband
seeks to forbid her to see Heathcliff again, Cathy bursts out in
contemptuous anger:

> '"Oh, for mercy's sake," interrupted the mistress, stamping her
> foot, "for mercy's sake, let us hear no more of it now! Your cold
> blood cannot be worked into a fever—your veins are full of ice-

Opposite above
Oakwell Hall: Charlotte praised in *Shirley* the foresight of painting the oak panels
of the drawing-room of Fieldhead as making the room more cheerful, and saving
the servants much toil.

Opposite below
Oakwell Hall – interior view.

Tree on Haworth Moor, wind-blown and misshapen, symbol of harsh struggle against the elements.
'The wild hillside, the winter morn
   The gnarled and ancient tree'
Emily Brontë, 'I knew not . . .'

water—but mine are boiling, and the sight of such chilliness makes them dance."

"To get rid of me—answer my question," persevered Mr Linton. "You *must* answer it; and that violence does not alarm me. I have found that you can be as stoical as anyone, when you please. Will you give up Heathcliff hereafter, or will you give up me? It is impossible for you to be *my* friend, and *his* at the same time; and I absolutely *require* to know which you choose."

"I require to be let alone!" exclaimed Catherine, furiously. "I demand it! Don't you see I can scarcely stand? Edgar, you—you leave me!"

She rung the bell till it broke with a twang: I entered leisurely. It was enough to try the temper of a saint, such senseless, wicked rages! There she lay dashing her head against the arm of the sofa, and grinding her teeth, so that you might fancy she would crash them to splinters!'

(*Wuthering Heights*, Chapter 11)

Cathy falls ill. In an intermediate condition between violence and calm she recalls the birds of the moors and Penistone Crag, based on that formidable ledge of high rock, Ponden Kirk, terrible in its silence and its magnitude. She is plucking feathers from the pillow which she has just torn with her teeth:

"'That's a turkey's," she murmured to herself; "and this is a wild duck's; and this is a pigeon's. Ah, they put pigeons' feathers in the pillows—no wonder I couldn't die! Let me take care to throw it on the floor when I lie down. And here's a moor-cock's; and this— I should know it among a thousand—it's a lapwing's. Bonny bird; wheeling over our heads in the middle of the moor. It wanted to get to its nest, for the clouds touched the swells, and it felt rain coming. This feather was picked up from the heath, the bird was not shot— we saw its nest in the winter, full of little skeletons. Heathcliff set a trap over it, and the old ones dare not come. I made him promise he'd never shoot a lapwing, after that, and he didn't. Yes, here are more! Did he shoot my lapwings, Nelly? Are they red, any of them? Let me look."

"Give over with that baby-work!" I interrupted, dragging the pillow away, and turning the holes towards the mattress, for she was removing its contents by handfuls. "Lie down and shut your eyes, you're wandering. There's a mess! The down is flying about like snow!"

I went here and there collecting it.

Trees line the footpath from Haworth village leading up to the moors.

"I see in you, Nelly," she continued, dreamily, "an aged woman—you have grey hair, and bent shoulders. This bed is the fairy cave under Penistone Crag, and you are gathering elf-bolts to hurt our heifers; pretending, while I am near, that they are only locks of wool. That's what you'll come to fifty years hence: I know you are not so now. I'm not wandering, you're mistaken, or else I should believe you really *were* that withered hag, and I should think I *was* under Penistone Crag, ...'"

(*Wuthering Heights*, Chapter 12)

But she wants to be there:

'Oh, I'm burning! I wish I were out of doors—I wish I were a girl again, half savage and hardy, and free ... and laughing at injuries, not maddening under them! Why am I so changed? ... I'm sure I should be myself were I once among the heather on those hills.'

(*Wuthering Heights*, Chapter 12)

Cathy jumps from her bed and looks through the window. She claims to see the lights of Wuthering Heights that were, in fact, never visible from Thrushcross. She calls to Heathcliff to come to her, but he has eloped with Linton's sister, Isabella, merely, be it said, in furtherance of his vengeance. In due course he returns to see the dying Cathy. It is a terrifying scene:

"'You and Edgar have broken my heart, Heathcliff! And you both come to bewail the deed to me, as if you were the people to be pitied! I shall not pity you, not I. You have killed me—and thriven on it, I think. How strong you are! How many years do you mean to live after I am gone?"

Heathcliff had knelt on one knee to embrace her; he attempted to rise, but she seized his hair, and kept him down.

"I wish I could hold you," she continued, bitterly, "till we were both dead! I shouldn't care what you suffered. I care nothing for your sufferings. Why shouldn't you suffer? I do." ...

"Don't torture me till I'm as mad as yourself," cried he, wrenching his head free, and grinding his teeth.

The two, to a cool spectator, made a strange and fearful picture. Well might Catherine deem that heaven would be a land of exile to her, unless, with her mortal body, she cast away her mortal character also. Her present countenance had a wild vindictiveness in its white cheek, and a bloodless lip, and scintillating eye; and she retained, in her closed fingers, a portion of the locks she had been grasping . . . .

"Are you possessed with a devil," he pursued, savagely, "to talk in that manner to me, when you are dying? Do you reflect that all those words will be branded in my memory, and eating deeper eternally, after you have left me? You know you lie to say I have killed you; and, Catherine, you know that I could as soon forget you, as my existence! Is it not sufficient for your infernal selfishness, that while you are at peace I shall writhe in the torments of hell?"

"I shall not be at peace," moaned Catherine, recalled to a sense of physical weakness by the violent, unequal throbbing of her heart, which beat visibly, and audibly, under this excess of agitation.'

(*Wuthering Heights*, Chapter 15)

Cathy was buried:

'. . . on a green slope, in a corner of the kirkyard, where the wall is so low that heath and bilberry plants have climbed over it from the moor; and peat mould almost buries it.'

(*Wuthering Heights*, Chapter 16)

It looks peaceful enough when at the end Lockwood visits the place, now the site of three graves:

'I sought, and soon discovered, the three headstones on the slope next the moor—the middle one, grey, and half buried in heath— Edgar Linton's only harmonized by the turf and moss, creeping up its foot—Heathcliff's still bare.

I lingered round them, under that benign sky; watched the moths fluttering among the heath and hare-bells; listened to the soft wind breathing through the grass; and wondered how anyone could ever imagine unquiet slumbers, for the sleepers in that quiet earth.'

(*Wuthering Heights*, Chapter 34)

It is Lockwood's earlier visit, however, that southern stranger on these northern moors, which many would consider more typical. 'Sky and hills mingled in one bitter whirl of wind and suffocating snow.' Returning next day across the moor ' . . . the whole hill-back was one billowy, white ocean.' Those hills can seem bleak enough in summer. That is what they are like in winter. They are indeed 'wuthering' heights.

7. The Belgian Experience

The Brontë sisters had to leave their beloved moors yet again. Neither literature nor governessing seemed to offer any tolerable future, so they hit upon another scheme. They would establish their own school. Aunt Branwell promised financial help and Miss Wooler was prepared to relinquish her establishment at Dewsbury Moor on favourable terms. The Whites, however, drew Charlotte's attention to the competitive problems of running a school and suggested that she should improve her qualifications by going abroad. First thoughts were of Brussels, then of Lille and then Brussels again. So in February 1842, with Emily, on a last and once more vain endeavour to separate herself from Haworth, Charlotte set off for what has been described as the biggest experience of her life, and out of which came much of *The Professor* and *Villette*.

The sisters were accompanied by their father and stayed at that quaint hostelry frequented mainly by parsons, the Chapter Coffee House in Paternoster Row. Though Lucy Snowe in *Villette* went alone, it is not unreasonable to assume that in many regards her fictional impressions derive from Charlotte's factual ones. Here is her first impression of London:

> 'The strange speech of the cabmen and others waiting round seemed to me odd as a foreign tongue. I had never before heard the English language chopped up in that way . . . . In London for the first time; at an inn for the first time; tired with travelling; confused with darkness; palsied with cold.'
>
> (*Villette*, Chapter 5)

The garden of the Pensionnat Heger. '. . . that old garden had its charms. . . . The turf was verdant, the gravelled walks were white; sun-bright nasturtiums clustered beautiful about the roots of the doddered orchard giants. There was a large berceau, above which spread the shade of an acacia; there was a smaller, more sequestered bower, nestled in the vines which ran all along a high and grey wall, . . . and hung in clusters . . . above the favoured spot where jasmine and ivy met and married them.' (*Villette*, Chapter 12)

Nevertheless, on the following day:

> 'Elation and pleasure were in my heart: to walk alone in London seemed of itself an adventure . . . I got into the heart of city life. I saw and felt London at last.'
>
> (*Villette*, Chapter 6)

Patrick and the girls took ship to the Continent. So did Lucy Snowe and, arriving on Belgian soil and travelling to Villette (ie Brussels), she provides a thumbnail sketch of the drab Netherlands countryside in late winter:

> 'Somewhat bare, flat and treeless was the route along which our

journey lay; and slimy canals crept, like half-torpid green snakes, beside the road; and formal pollard willows edged level fields, tilled like kitchen garden beds.'

(*Villette*, Chapter 7)

A far cry from the Yorkshire moors! Poor Emily!

They arrived in Brussels and stayed one night with Mr and Mrs Jenkins, he being the chaplain at the British Embassy. Patrick stayed on for several days, but the girls proceeded to the Pensionnat Heger in the rue d'Isabelle (the rue Fossette of *Villette*), which housed some forty day pupils and twelve boarders.

Both house and street have now disappeared beneath a complex of new buildings. The house was divided by a large hall or *carré* with the private rooms of the Heger family on the right and the classrooms and refectory on the left. Opposite the street door of the hall was the glass-covered 'Galerie' which spread onto the garden and, separately, to the stone-flagged playground. On the further side of these and squaring the quadrangle was the main classroom with the dormitory above. The front and back parts of the house were joined by the long refectory.

It was the high-walled garden, however, which appealed most to Charlotte. This is surely hers as much as Lucy Snowe's expression of delight:

'Independently of romantic rubbish, however, that old garden had its charms. On summer mornings I used to rise early to enjoy them alone; on summer evenings, to linger solitary, to keep tryste with the rising moon, or taste one kiss of the evening breeze, or fancy rather than feel the freshness of dew descending. The turf was verdant, the gravelled walks were white; sun-bright nasturtiums clustered beautiful about the roots of the doddered orchard giants. There was a large berceau, above which spread the shade of an acacia; there was a smaller, more sequestered bower, nestled in the vines which ran all along a high and grey wall, and gathered their tendrils in a knot of beauty, and hung their clusters in loving profusion about the favoured spot where jasmine and ivy met and married them.'

(*Villette*, Chapter 12)

Charlotte did not much like the pupils she found here, any more indeed than those she had tried to teach in England. 'Mutinous and difficult for the teachers to manage;' she wrote in July 1842, 'and their principles are rotten to the core.' On 6 March 1843 when she had returned to Brussels alone after coming home for Aunt Branwell's funeral she told Ellen Nussey, 'M and Madame Heger are the only two persons in the house for whom I really experience regard and esteem.' She had returned not merely as pupil but now also as instructress in English to Monsieur Heger and his brother-in-law.

A month later, however, Charlotte was complaining of 'privations and humiliations ... monotony and uniformity of life; and, above all, there is a constant sense of solitude in the midst of numbers.' She particularized: 'The Protestant, the foreigner, is a solitary being.' Life became lonelier and the long vacation that summer was a trial:

> 'I have nothing to tell you. One day is like another in this place. I know you, living in the country, can hardly believe it is possible life can be monotonous in the centre of a brilliant capital like Brussels; but so it is. I feel it most on holidays, when all the girls and teachers go out to visit, and it sometimes happens that I am left, during several hours, quite alone, with four great desolate school-rooms at my disposition. I try to read, I try to write; but in vain. I then wander about from room to room, but the silence and loneliness of all the house weighs down one's spirits like lead.'
>
> (*Life*, Chapter 12)

This staunch Protestant was reduced in her despair to going to a confessional with a Catholic priest. In a letter of 2 September 1843 she told Emily about it:

> 'An odd whim came into my head. In a solitary part of the Cathedral six or seven people still remained kneeling by the confessionals. In two confessionals I saw a priest. I felt as if I did not care what I did, provided it was not absolutely wrong, and that it served to vary my life and yield a moment's interest. I took a fancy to change myself into a Catholic and go and make a real confession to see what it was like. Knowing me as you do, you will think this odd, but when people are by themselves they have singular fancies. A penitent was occupied in confessing. They do not go into the sort of pew or cloister which the priest occupies, but kneel down on the steps and confess through a grating. Both the confessor and the penitent whisper very low, you can hardly hear their voices. After I had watched two or three penitents go and return, I approached at last and knelt down in a niche which was just vacated. I had to kneel there ten minutes waiting, for on the other side was another penitent invisible to me. At last that went away and a little wooden door inside the grating opened, and I saw the priest leaning his ear towards me. I was obliged to begin, and yet I did not know a word of the formula with which they always commence their confessions. It

was a funny position. I felt precisely as I did when alone on the Thames at midnight. I commenced with saying I was a foreigner and had been brought up a Protestant. The priest asked if I was a Protestant then. I somehow could not tell a lie, and said "yes". He replied that in that case I could not "jouir du bonheur de la confesse"; but I was determined to confess, and at last he said he would allow me because it might be the first step towards returning to the true church. I actually did confess—a real confession. When I had done he told me his address, and said that every morning I was to go to the rue du Parc—to his house—and he would reason with me and try to convince me of the error and enormity of being a Protestant !!! I promised faithfully to go. Of course, however, the adventure stops there, and I hope I shall never see the priest again. I think you had better not tell papa of this. He will not understand that it was only a freak, and will perhaps think I am going to turn Catholic. . . .'

What had happened to Charlotte? Why was she so intensely lonely? Above all else, Madame Heger's attitude had changed. Mrs Gaskell attributed it to the clash of Protestant and Catholic dévotees, but there was more than that and Mrs Gaskell knew there was. Monsieur Heger Charlotte had described to Ellen Nussey in a letter of 5 May 1842 as:

'. . . a man of power as to mind, but very choleric and irritable as to temperament, a little black ugly being, with a face that varies in expression.'

She had fallen in love with him. The story is told vicariously in Lucy Snowe's attraction to Monsieur Paul Emanuel, expressed as desire for a fraternal relationship:

"'Is monsieur quite serious? Does he really think he needs me, and can take an interest in me as a sister?"

"Surely, surely," said he, "a lonely man like me, who has no sister, must be but too glad to find in some woman's heart a sister's pure affection."

"And dare I rely on monsieur's regard? Dare I speak to him when I am so inclined?"

"My little sister must make her own experiments," said he; "I will give no promises. She must tease and try her wayward brother till she has drilled him into what she wishes. After all, he is no inductile material in some hands."

While he spoke, the tone of his voice, the light of his now

The rue d'Isabelle and the Pensionnat Heger with the church of St Gudule in the background. 'In a very quiet and comparatively clean and well paved street . . . a rather large house, loftier by a storey than those round it.' (*Villette*, Chapter 8)

affectionate eye, gave me such a pleasure as, certainly, I had never felt. I envied no girl her lover, no bride her bridegroom, no wife her husband; I was content with this my voluntary, self-offering friend. If he would but prove reliable, and he *looked* reliable, what, beyond his friendship, could I ever covet? But, if all melted like a dream, as once before had happened—? . . .

"Why were you so glad to be friends with M Paul?" asks the reader. "Had he not long been a friend to you? Had he not given proof on proof of a certain partiality in his feelings?"

Yes, he had; but still I liked to hear him say so earnestly—that he was my close, true friend; I liked his modest doubts, his tender deference—that trust which longed to rest, and was grateful when taught how. He had called me "sister". It was well. Yes; he might call me what he pleased, so long as he confided in me. I was willing to be his sister, on condition that he did not invite me to fill that relation to some future wife of his; and tacitly vowed as he was to celibacy, of this dilemma there seemed little danger.'

(*Villette*, Chapters 35, 36)

Madame Heger realized what was happening. Charlotte detected a cooling of feelings and much of her dislike of Madame Heger was later distilled into the creation of Madame Beck, the black eminence of *Villette*. On 15 November 1843 Charlotte told Ellen Nussey 'I fancy I begin to perceive the reason of this mighty distance and reserve; it sometimes makes me laugh, and at other times nearly cry.' She was back home before the end of the year, and she then recorded 'However long I live, I shall not forget what the parting with M Heger cost me.'

The measure of that parting is in the letters that Charlotte subsequently wrote and that Mrs Gaskell saw and would not, no doubt because she thought she could not, publish.

Only four have survived, the last of them from 18 November 1845. The sentiments expressed in that of 9 January 1845 are representative:

> 'Day and night I find neither rest nor peace. If I sleep I am disturbed by tormenting dreams in which I see you, always severe, always grave, always incensed against me.
>
> Forgive me then, Monsieur, if I adopt the course of writing to you again. How can I endure life if I make no effort to ease its sufferings? . . .
>
> All I know is, that I cannot, that I will not, resign myself to lose wholly the friendship of my master. I would rather suffer the greatest physical pain than always have my heart lacerated by smarting regrets. If my master withdraws his friendship from me entirely I shall be altogether without hope; if he gives me a little— just a little—I shall be satisfied—happy; I shall have a reason for living on, for working.'

Although written some years before, one of Charlotte's poems aptly expresses her desolation at this time:

> 'Unloved—I love; unwept—I weep;
> Grief I restrain—hope I repress:
> Vain is the anguish—fixed and deep;
> Vainer, desires and dreams of bliss—
>
> My love awakes no love again,
> My tears collect, and fall unfelt;
> My sorrow touches none with pain,
> My humble hopes to nothing melt.

For me the universe is dumb,
Stone-deaf, and blank, and wholly blind;
Life I must bound, existence sum
In the strait limits of one mind;

That mind my own. Oh! narrow cell;
Dark—imageless—a living tomb!
There must I sleep, there wake and dwell
Content, with palsy, pain, and gloom.'

8. Haworth Again, Hathersage and Authorship

Charlotte was back at home with Emily, and so by July 1845 were Anne and Branwell. Anne had decided not to return to her work with the Robinsons at Thorp Green. She left on 11 June; Branwell, departing some five weeks later, did not get the choice. He received a letter from Mr Robinson bidding him 'break off instantly and for ever all communication with every member of his family.' Whether it was a case, as Patrick Brontë described Mrs Gaskell's portrayal of the relationship of Branwell and Mrs Robinson, of 'my brilliant and unhappy son and of his diabolical seducer', whether these two were, as Branwell claimed, really in love with each other, or whether there were other reasons for Mr Robinson's peremptory and decisive action, we shall never know for certain. It is hard to believe Branwell. This, however, proved to be the end. Whatever his profligacy before, it was as nothing to the alcoholic and drug-addicted decline that followed.

Charlotte heard the news of Branwell's dismissal when she returned from a fortnight spent with Ellen Nussey preparing the vicarage at Hathersage (Derbyshire) for her former suitor, Henry Nussey, and his new bride. One is tempted to think that the description in *Jane Eyre* (and there are Eyre tombs in Hathersage Church) of the refurbishing of Moor House may have had its parallel in the activities of Charlotte and Ellen at the vicarage:

Opposite
Kirk Smeaton Church where Arthur Bell Nicholls became curate to the rich absentee rector, Thomas Cator, after Patrick Brontë reacted with such hostility to his proposal of marriage to Charlotte.

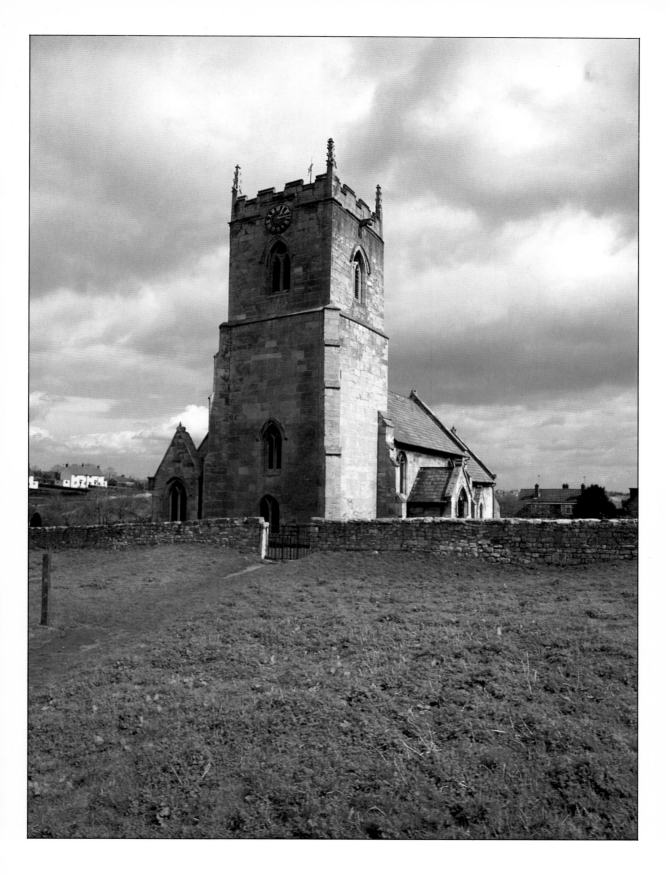

Windermere where at the
Kay-Shuttleworth's house,
Briery Close, Charlotte first
met Mrs Gaskell.

The grandeur of mountain and water in the Lake District.

Autumn browns on the moors.
'Forests of heather, dark and long,
Wave their brown branching arms above . . .'
Emily Brontë, 'I've seen this dell . . .'

'Happy at Moor House I was, and hard I worked; and so did Hannah: she was charmed to see how jovial I could be amidst the bustle of a house turned topsy turvy—how I could brush, and dust, and clean, and cook. And really, after a day or two of confusion worse confounded, it was delightful by degrees to invoke order from the chaos ourselves had made. I had previously taken a journey to S—— to purchase some new furniture: my cousins having given me *carte blanche* to effect what alterations I pleased, and a sum having been set aside for that purpose. The ordinary sitting-room and bedrooms I left much as they were; for I knew Diana and Mary would derive more pleasure from seeing again the old homely tables and chairs and beds, than from the spectacle of the smartest innovations. Still some novelty was necessary, to give to their return the piquancy with which I wished it to be invested. Dark handsome new carpets and curtains, an arrangement of some carefully selected antique ornaments in porcelain and bronze, new coverings, and mirrors, and dressing-cases, for the toilet tables, answered the end: they looked fresh without being glaring. A spare parlour and bedroom I refurnished entirely, with old mahogany and crimson upholstery; I laid canvas on the passage, and carpets on the stairs. When all was finished, I thought Moor House as complete a model of bright, modest snugness within, as it was, at this season, a specimen of wintry waste and desert dreariness without.'

(*Jane Eyre*, Chapter 34)

Some indeed have claimed that Moor House is based on Hathersage Vicarage and that the description of the surrounding landscape is based on Charlotte's recollections of the Peak District:

'They loved their sequestered home. I, too, in the grey, small, antique structure, with its low roof, its latticed casements, its mouldering walls, its avenue of aged firs—all grown aslant under the stress of mountain winds; its garden, dark with yew and holly—and where no flowers but of the hardiest species would bloom—found a charm both potent and permanent. They clung to the purple moors behind and around their dwelling—to the hollow vale into which the pebbly bridle-path leading from their gate descended, and which wound between fern-banks first, and then amongst a few of the wildest little pasture fields that ever bordered a wilderness of heath, or gave sustenance to a flock of grey moorland sheep, with their little mossy-faced lambs—they clung to this scene, I say, with a perfect enthusiasm of attachment. I could comprehend the feeling, and share both its strength and truth. I saw the fascination of the

Hathersage Vicarage which Ellen and Charlotte prepared for Henry Nussey's occupation, as Jane Eyre prepared Moor House for Diana and Mary Rivers.

locality. I felt the consecration of its loneliness: my eye feasted on the outline of swell and sweep—on the wild colouring communicated to ridge and dell by moss, by heath-bell, by flower-sprinkled turf, by brilliant bracken, and mellow granite crag.'

(*Jane Eyre*, Chapter 30)

Indeed the situation at this time seems also to have encompassed Charlotte's envisaging her sisters in the appearance of Diana and Mary Rivers, even to the animals and especially the dog, probably Keeper, of whom Emily was in her own way so strangely fond:

'Two young, graceful women—ladies in every point—sat, one in a low rocking-chair, the other on a lower stool; both wore deep mourning of crape and bombazeen, which sombre garb singularly set off very fair necks and faces: a large old pointer dog rested its massive head on the knee of one girl; in the lap of the other was cushioned a black cat. . . . I cannot call them handsome—they were too pale and grave for the word; as they each bent over a book, they

Rooks in Haworth churchyard with the parsonage beyond.

Braemoor between Thornton
Heath and Haworth.
'A heaven so clear, an earth so calm,
So sweet, so soft, so hushed an air'
Emily Brontë, 'A little while . . .'

looked thoughtful almost to severity. . . . Both were fair complex-
ioned and slenderly made; both possessed faces full of distinction
and intelligence. One, to be sure, had hair a shade darker than the
other, and there was a difference in their style of wearing it: Mary's
pale brown locks were parted and braided smooth; Diana's duskier
tresses covered her neck with thick curls.'

(*Jane Eyre*, Chapter 28)

The three sisters, now together once again, revived the idea of running a
school. They had Aunt Branwell's money to assist them and were
prepared to use her old bedroom as a dormitory and the sitting-cum-
dining-room as a schoolroom. A prospectus was printed, people were
written to, but the result was a total lack of response. Charlotte,
however, moved in a quite different direction after finding some of
Emily's verses in manuscript. At the beginning of 1846 she offered the
poems of Currer, Ellis and Acton Bell to Aylott and Jones, who accepted
to publish at the authors' expense. The pseudonyms were used to cover
the possible disadvantages of the female sex, though with the prolifer-
ation of women writers in the period there would seem to have been little
need for the subterfuge. Few copies of the *Poems* were sold.

Charlotte asked the publishers if they were interested in novels, but
they were not. So *Wuthering Heights* (by Emily), *Agnes Grey* (by Anne)
and *The Professor* based extensively on the Belgian experiences (by
Charlotte) were submitted to six other publishers before Newby
accepted the first two and published them in December 1847. He rejected
The Professor, so Charlotte submitted it to Smith, Elder, who, though
rejecting it also, encouraged her to submit anything else she might write.
Jane Eyre was ready, promptly submitted, accepted and published in
October 1847, two months ahead of her sisters' works and running to a
second edition, with a dedication to Thackeray, in January 1848.

Mrs Gaskell tells the story of Charlotte's revealing her first success as
an author to her father:

'When the demand for the work had assured success to *Jane Eyre*,
her sisters urged Charlotte to tell their father of its publication. She
accordingly went into his study one afternoon after his early dinner,
carrying with her a copy of the book, and one or two reviews, taking
care to include a notice adverse to it.

She informed me that something like the following conversation
took place between her and him. (I wrote down her words the day
after I heard them; and I am pretty sure they are quite accurate.)

"Papa, I've been writing a book."

"Have you, my dear?"

"Yes, and I want you to read it."

"I am afraid it will try my eyes too much."

"But it is not in manuscript: it is printed."

"My dear! you've never thought of the expense it will be! It will be almost sure to be a loss, for how can you get a book sold? No one knows you or your name!"

"But, papa, I don't think it will be a loss; no more will you, if you will just let me read you a review or two, and tell you more about it."

So she sat down and read some of the reviews to her father; and then, giving him the copy of *Jane Eyre* that she intended for him, she left him to read it. When he came in to tea, he said, "Girls, do you know Charlotte has been writing a book, and it is much better than likely?"'

(*Life*, Chapter 16)

The unscrupulous Newby brought out Anne's second novel, *The Tenant of Wildfell Hall*, in July 1848, advertizing it in such a way as to imply that it was by the author of *Wuthering Heights* and *Jane Eyre*. This attempt to conflate three sisters into one caused some consternation at Smith, Elder, who were dealing with Charlotte for a second novel, and it took a visit to London by her and Anne to convince her publishers that the Brontë sisters (or Bells) were plural and not singular. The careers of the Brontë sisters as novelists had begun—and for Emily and Anne had ended.

9. The 'Shirley' Country

Charlotte Brontë's two novels after *Jane Eyre* took her back—*Villette* to the Belgian period and *Shirley* partly to her own stay in the Dewsbury area but partly also drawing on her father's memories. In a sense the Brontë story comes full circle in going back to that place and those times when Patrick first found himself in Yorkshire. The writing of *Shirley* took place in the midst of personal bereavement. That may be why there is such a reminiscent air about it. Some have detected—Mrs Gaskell among them—in the proud, independent spirit of Shirley Keeldar a fictional re-creation of Emily. Ellen Nussey believed that much of herself had gone into Caroline Helstone, and the curates are undoubtedly a gloriously wicked set of caricatures of some who had appeared, and not always in the most welcome circumstances, at Haworth Parsonage. Clearest of all, however, is the portrayal of the Taylor family as the Yorkes and, based probably on her father's memories, of Hammond Roberson, that incarnation of the Church Militant, in Matthewson Helstone.

For her setting Charlotte goes back to 1812 and the ill-conceived Luddite riots which ravaged much of the Yorkshire woollen district at the time. This uprising was directed principally against William Cartwright, the owner of Rawfolds Mill, Liversedge, who in 1809 had introduced the new shearing or cropping machines which gave to the woollen cloth an attractive smooth finish. So successful were these machines that he decided to purchase yet more. The croppers decided to stop this. They discussed their plans at the Shears Inn (still to be seen in Halifax Road, Hightown). The new machines were destroyed in transit over Hartshead Moor. An attack on the mill itself was decided upon. Cartwright had taken precautions. Four workmen and five soldiers were with him in the mill and other soldiers were billeted in the district. Haigh

Rawfolds Mill, the actual mill which the Luddites attacked, now no longer in existence, though one shed was later incorporated into Rigby's Wire Works. The mill was owned by William Cartwright, whose installation of new machinery in 1809 helped cause the riots. The street near which the mill was sited is still Cartwright Street.

Hall, not far from the Shears Inn, was the 'battle' headquarters of the soldiery. The attack came on the night of Saturday, 11 April 1812. The force of about 150 Luddites moved from the area of Roe Head School, over the fields and lanes, along the old Roman road across the bridge over the Spen, to the mill gates. Their assault on the mill was met by rifle fire from the upper storeys. The factory bell boomed, calling the soldiery from around to its defence. After half an hour all was over. Cartwright was victorious before the soldiers arrived. The rebels fled with two of their number left dying in the millyard.

The fictional version has Shirley and Caroline watching in terror:

"'Shirley—Shirley, the gates are down! That crash was like the felling of great trees. Now they are pouring through.'' ...
"They come on!" cried Shirley. "How steadily they march in! There is discipline in their ranks—I will not say there is courage: hundreds against tens are no proof of that quality; but" (she dropped her voice) "there is suffering and desperation enough amongst them—these goads will urge them forwards." ... A

crash—smash—shiver—stopped their whispers. A simultaneously hurled volley of stones had saluted the broad front of the mill, with all its windows; and now every pane of every lattice lay in shattered and pounded fragments. A yell followed this demonstration—a rioters' yell—a North-of-England—a Yorkshire—a West-Riding—a West-Riding-clothing-district-of-Yorkshire rioters' yell. . . . What was going on now? It seemed difficult, in the darkness, to distinguish; but something terrible, a still-renewing tumult, was obvious—fierce attacks, desperate repulses. The millyard, the mill itself, was full of battle movement; there was scarcely any cessation now of the discharge of firearms, and there was struggling, rushing, trampling, and shouting between. The aim of the assailants seemed to be to enter the mill, that of the defenders to beat them off. They heard the rebel leader cry, "To the back, lads!" They heard a voice retort, "Come, round, we will meet you!"

"To the counting-house!" was the order again.

"Welcome! We shall have you there!" was the response. And, accordingly, the fiercest blaze that had yet glowed, the loudest rattle that had yet been heard, burst from the counting-house front, when the mass of rioters rushed up to it.

The voice that had spoken was Moore's own voice. They could tell by its tones that his soul was now warm with the conflict; they could guess that the fighting animal was roused in every one of those men there struggling together, and was for the time quite paramount above the rational human being. . . . Moore had expected this attack for days, perhaps weeks; he was prepared for it at every point. He had fortified and garrisoned his mill, which in itself was a strong building; he was a cool, brave man: he stood to the defence with unflinching firmness. Those who were with him caught his spirit and copied his demeanour. The rioters had never been so met before. At other mills they had attacked they had found no resistance; an organized, resolute defence was what they never dreamed of encountering. When their leaders saw the steady fire kept up from the mill, witnessed the composure and determination of its owner, heard themselves coolly defied and invited on to death, and beheld their men falling wounded round them, they felt that nothing was to be done here. In haste, they mustered their forces, drew them away from the building; a roll was called over, in which the men answered to figures instead of names; they dispersed wide over the fields, leaving silence and ruin behind them. The attack, from its commencement to its termination, had not occupied an hour.

Day was by this time approaching; the west was dim, the east beginning to gleam. It would have seemed that the girls who had

Hammond Roberson, incumbent of Liversedge, a leading Yorkshire Evangelical,
on whom Matthewson Helstone in *Shirley* was based.

watched this conflict would now wish to hasten to the victors, on
whose side all their interest had been enlisted; but they only very
cautiously approached the now battered mill, and when suddenly a
number of soldiers and gentlemen appeared at the great door
opening into the yard, they quickly stepped aside into a shed, the
deposit of old iron and timber, whence they could see without being
seen.

It was no cheering spectacle; these premises were now a mere
blot of desolation on the fresh front of the summer-dawn. All the
copse up the Hollow was shady and dewy; the hill at its head was
green; but just here in the centre of the sweet glen, Discord, broken
loose in the night from control, had beaten the ground with his
stamping hoofs, and left it waste and pulverized. The mill yawned

all ruinous with unglazed frames; the yard was thickly bestrewn with stones and brickbats; and, close under the mill, with the glittering fragments of the shattered windows, muskets and other weapons lay here and there; more than one deep crimson stain was visible on the gravel; a human body lay quiet on its face near the gates; and five or six wounded men writhed and moaned in the bloody dust.'

(*Shirley*, Chapter 19)

At the time of the riots Patrick Brontë was incumbent of Hartshead. He denounced the murderous vandalism, and so did Hammond Roberson who lived at Heald's Hall nearby. The ringleaders were arrested, tried at York and condemned. Several of them were hanged and more transported. A few years later in 1816 Roberson at his own expense (£7,474—carefully recorded) built Liversedge Church. As is said to have been claimed of another such building erected amid similar circumstances, conditions showed that a church was 'much needed and might do some good.'

Rawfolds Mill has disappeared, but it may not in any case have been the physical model for the Hollows. That, it has been suggested (by Erskine Stuart, *The Brontë Country*, 1888, p 146) was, in fact, Hunsworth Mill, near Cleckheaton, which had been owned by the Taylor family. This is set in a valley such as that Charlotte described Caroline and Mrs Pryor walking along:

'Here the opposing sides of the glen approaching each other, and becoming clothed with brushwood and stunted oaks, formed a wooded ravine, at the bottom of which ran the mill-stream, in broken unquiet course, struggling with many stones, chafing against rugged banks, fretting with gnarled tree-roots, foaming, gurgling, battling as it went. Here, when you had wandered half a mile from the mill, you found a sense of deep solitude; found it in the shade of unmolested trees; received it in the singing of many birds, for which that shade made a home. This was no trodden way; the freshness of the wood-flowers attested that foot of man seldom pressed them; the abounding wild-roses looked as if they budded, bloomed, and faded under the watch of solitude, as in a sultan's harem. Here you saw the sweet azure of bluebells, and recognized in pearl-white blossoms, spangling the grass, a humble type of some star-lit spot in space.'

(*Shirley*, Chapter 21)

Opposite
Heald's Hall, Liversedge, home of Hammond Robertson.

By 1888 things were different:

> 'The Hollows is like this still, only it is soot grimed, and in the immediate neighbourhood are railways, factories, blast furnaces and mines, while into the beck the Oakenshaw and Hunsworth Mills excrete a deep logwood and indigo mixture.'
>
> (*The Brontë Country*, p 148)

The Hollow now lies in close proximity to the M62 motorway.

The 'Shirley' country, however, had vivid memories, not just for her father but for Charlotte as well. Besides Miss Wooler's school at Roe Head and Dewsbury Moor and Ellen Nussey's home at Rydings, there were other familiar places like the Taylors' Red House at Gomersal (Briarmains of the novel), Oakwell Hall (Fieldhead), Nunnely Park and Nunnwood (Kirklees Park) and Briarfield Church (Birstall).

Many significant events in *Shirley* are acted out in the setting of Briarfield Church, including Shirley and Caroline hiding in the church-yard during the attack on the mill, and the dual marriage ceremony at the end of the novel. The present building is not the one that Charlotte Brontë knew. As a result of large-scale restoration, it dates from around

Red House, Gomersal, built in 1660 of brick—unusual in those days—hence its name, and little changed since then.

Hunsworth Mill, built in 1785 and owned by the Taylors, the model for Moore's mill in *Shirley*, where woollen cloth was woven, processed and dyed, the latter causing river pollution.

1870, when the vicar, coming near to the end of nearly forty years in the parish, was William Margetson Heald, usually identified as the prototype of one of the curates, Cyril Hall, in the novel.

The other ecclesiastical building, Briar Chapel, the resort of the ranters, 'a large, new, raw Wesleyan place of worship' (*Shirley*, Chapter 9) was built in 1827 just behind Red House Croft. It has always been known locally with typical Yorkshire forthrightness, even irreverence, as 'Pork Pie Chapel' because of its shape.

The Red House dates from 1660. Its warm-hearted, lively minded family became very dear to Charlotte: '... the society of the Taylors is one of the most rousing pleasures I have known.' (*Brontë Society Transactions*, 1944, p 215) This, despite her Toryism and their radicalism. Indeed, she makes something of this difference in *Shirley* in the encounters of Mr Yorke and Helstone.

Winifred Gérin has described the house as:

> '... a long and low structure, only two stories high, with high French windows reaching to the ground in front, five gables at the rear trellised and covered with creepers, and surrounded back and front by lawns.'
>
> (*Charlotte Brontë: The Evolution of Genius*, 1967, p 71)

Charlotte Brontë says little about the outside beyond mentioning 'the great trees, strong-trunked and broad-armed, which guarded the gable nearest the road', but she does describe the back parlour farthest to the right where the evening discussions took place:

> 'This is the usual sitting-room of an evening. Those windows would be seen by daylight to be of brilliantly stained glass—purple and amber the predominant hues, glittering round a gravely tinted medallion in the centre of each, representing the suave head of William Shakespeare and the serene one of John Milton. Some Canadian views hang on the walls—green forest and blue water scenery—and in the midst of them blazes a night eruption of Vesuvius; very ardently it glows, contrasted with the cool foam and azure of cataracts and the dusky depths of woods.'
>
> (*Shirley*, Chapter 9)

The windows are preserved at the Brontë Parsonage Museum, the pictures are still to be seen at the Red House which with its Luddite relics is now open to visitors.

Charlotte seems to have been especially impressed by the evidence of the culture the house displayed. Elsewhere she writes:

'There was no splendour, but there was taste everywhere—unusual taste—the taste, you would have said, of a travelled man, a scholar, and a gentleman. A series of Italian views decked the walls; each of these was a specimen of true art; a connoisseur had selected them; they were genuine and valuable . . . . The subjects were all pastoral, the scenes were all sunny. There was a guitar and some music on a sofa; there were cameos, beautiful miniatures; a set of Grecian-looking vases on the mantelpiece; there were books well arranged in two elegant bookcases.'

(*Shirley*, Chapter 3)

The other important house of the novel is Fieldhead, the home of Shirley herself. It is based on the sixteenth-century manor house, Oakwell Hall, about half a mile from Birstall Church. As Charlotte describes it, 'This was neither a grand nor a comfortable house; within as without it was antique, rambling and incommodious.' It was allowed, however, to be picturesque:

'Its irregular architecture, and the grey and mossy colouring communicated by time, gave it just a claim to this epithet. The old latticed windows, the stone porch, the walls, the roof, the chimney stacks were rich in crayon touches and sepia lights and shades. The trees behind were fine, bold and spreading; the cedar on the lawn in front was grand, and the granite urns on the garden wall, the fretted arch of the gateway, were, for an artist, as the very desire of the eye.'

(*Shirley*, Chapter 11)

In the vestibule:

'Very sombre it was—long, vast and dark; one latticed window lit it but dimly. The wide old chimney contained no fire . . . . The gallery on high, opposite the entrance, was seen but in outline, so shadowy became this hall towards its ceiling; carved stags' heads with real antlers, looked down grotesquely from the walls . . . . The brown-panelled parlour was furnished all in old style, and with real old furniture. On each side of the mantelpiece stood two antique chairs of oak.'

(*Shirley*, Chapter 11)

Opposite above
Imposing Gawthorpe Hall near Burnley, home of Sir James and Lady Kay-Shuttleworth. This ancestral home of the Shuttleworths contains an outstanding collection of lace, embroidery and textiles.

Opposite below
Gawthorpe – the tree-lined approach to the late Elizabethan mansion, which was redesigned in the Victorian period.

Scarborough, where Anne
died and was buried and
where Miss Wooler had a
house in North Bay.

Of that panelling Charlotte Brontë allowed herself a mildly humorous, practical housewifely remark when contrasting it with the 'barbarous peach-bloom salon':

'Very handsome, reader, these shining brown panels are—very mellow in colouring and tasteful in effect—but, if you know what a 'spring clean' is, very execrable and inhuman. Whoever, having the bowels of humanity, has seen servants scrubbing at these polished wooden walls with beeswaxed cloths on a warm May day must allow that they are "intolerable, and not to be endured"; and I cannot but secretly applaud the benevolent barbarian who had painted another and larger apartment of Fieldhead—the drawing-room, to wit, formerly also an oak room—of a delicate pinky-white, thereby earning for himself the character of a Hun, but mightily enhancing the cheerfulness of that portion of his abode, and saving future housemaids a world of toil.'

(*Shirley*, Chapter 11)

These ancient abodes of Oakwell and the Red House (or Fieldhead and Briarmains, if you prefer it) were set in an ancient land:

'On Nunnwood—the sole remnant of antique British forest in a region whose lowlands were once all sylvan chase, as its highlands were breast-deep heather—slept the shadow of a cloud; the distant hills were dappled, the horizon was shaded and tinted like mother-of-pearl; silvery blues, soft purples, evanescent greens and rose-shades, all melting into fleeces of white cloud, pure as azury snow, allured the eye as with a remote glimpse of heaven's foundations.'

(*Shirley*, Chapter 12)

Nunnely and Nunnwood of the novel, associated with the real Kirklees Park, are redolent with history:

'"It is like an encampment of forest sons of Anak. The trees are huge and old. When you stand at their roots, the summits seem in another region, the trunks remain still and firm as pillars, while the boughs sway to every breeze. In the deepest calm their leaves are never quite hushed, and in high wind a flood rushes—a sea thunders above you."

"Was it not one of Robin Hood's haunts?"

Opposite
Upper Ponden, along the path between Ponden Hall and Ponden Kirk.
'The far hills cunningly kiss
That grey and sunless heaven above,
All dim and chilled, a time of tears,
And dying hopes and gathering fears.'
Charlotte Brontë, 'It is not at an hour like this'

"Yes, and there are mementos of him still existing. To penetrate into Nunnwood, Miss Keeldar, is to go far back into the dim days of eld. Can you see a break in the forest, about the centre?"

"Yes, distinctly."

"That break is a dell—a deep, hollow cup, lined with turf as green and short as the sod of this Common—the very oldest of the trees, gnarled mighty oaks, crowd about the brink of this dell; in the bottom lie the ruins of a nunnery.'"

(Shirley, Chapter 12)

The supposed grave of Robin Hood is there, and there had been a nunnery in the medieval period. From a nunnery to Luddites—very different; from Robin Hood to Luddites maybe not quite so different!

Just before this dialogue the two girls, Shirley Keeldar and Caroline Helstone, have been speaking of their origins. Caroline asks:

"'You are a Yorkshire girl, too?"

"I am—Yorkshire in blood and birth. Five generations of my race sleep under the aisles of Briarfield Church; I drew my first breath in the old black hall behind us.'"

Robert Moore himself, though having a Belgian mother, is reminded by Joe Scott:

"'But your father [and that would be pronounced with a short 'a'!] war Yorkshire, which maks ye a bit Yorkshire too: and onybody may see ye're akin to us, ye're so keen o' making brass and getting forrards.'"

(Shirley, Chapter 5)

Shirley is full of 'characters' and full of Yorkshire. They may not all originate from Yorkshire, but they all display that county's reputation for firmness of character and forthrightness of expression. Their loyalties and their animosities are alike formidable. Parson Helstone knows his mind and his course, and Robert Moore no less. But Mr Yorke, as his name implies, is the quintessential 'tyke':

'[He] is proud of his race. Yorkshire has such families here and there amongst her hills and wolds—peculiar, racy, vigorous; of good blood and strong brain; turbulent somewhat in the pride of their strength, and intractable in the force of their native powers; wanting polish, wanting consideration, wanting docility, but sound, spirited, and true-bred as the eagle on the cliff or the steed in the steppe.'

(Shirley, Chapter 9)

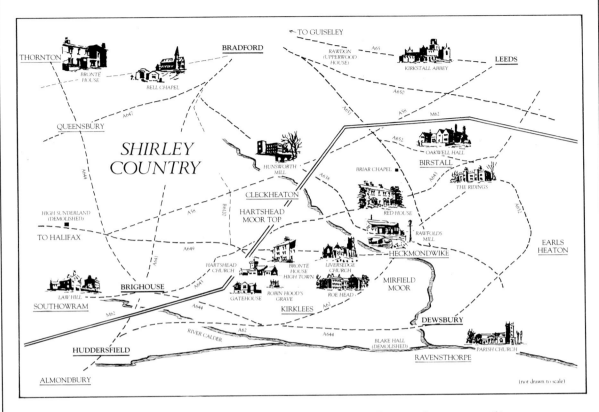

SHIRLEY COUNTRY

(not drawn to scale)

Yorke delights in the candour of his radical dissent from prevailing opinions. His reaction to the attack on Hollows Mill, on a visit to Parson Helstone's rectory, is typical:

'Mr Yorke was in no mild mood, and in no measured terms did he express his opinion on the transaction of the night; Moore, the magistrates, the soldiers, the mob-leaders, each and all came in for a share of his invectives, but he reserved his strongest epithets—and real racy Yorkshire Doric adjectives they were—for the benefit of the fighting parsons, the "sanguinary, demoniac" Rector and curate. According to him, the cup of ecclesiastical guilt was now full indeed.'

(*Shirley*, Chapter 21)

But Shirley with her masculine mind and temper returns him as good as he gives. She puts it in a county context:

'"I have sat on Jessy's stool by your chair in the back-parlour at Briarmains, for evenings together, listening excitedly to your talk, half admiring what you said, and half rebelling against it. I think you a fine old Yorkshireman, sir: I am proud to have been born in the same county and parish as yourself. Truthful, upright, independent you are, as a rock based below seas; but also you are harsh, rude, narrow, and merciless."

"Not to the poor, lass, nor to the meek of the earth: only to the proud and high-minded."

"And what right have you, sir, to make such distinctions? A prouder, a higher-minded man than yourself does not exist. You find it easy to speak comfortably to your inferiors; you are too haughty, too ambitious, too jealous to be civil to those above you.'"

(*Shirley*, Chapter 21)

To all of which Yorke, with that plain Yorkshire outspokenness, concludes, 'The Lord save us! Whoever weds thee must look about him!' The latter part of the novel is much occupied with proposals of marriage to Shirley—the one she quickly dismisses from Sam Wynne, the one she had rejected from Robert Moore, the one she rejects from Sir Philip Nunnely, the one she accepts (and it is a bit difficult for us to accept it) from Robert Moore's brother, tutor to her relatives, the Sympsons, Louis Moore. He hardly seems a match for Shirley, but then nor does the quiet, retiring Caroline for his brother, Robert.

But the narrator's old housekeeper has a word for it at the end: 'This world has queer changes.' She goes on to reflect on the changes in the Hollows landscape:

"'I can remember the old mill being built—the very first it was in all the district; and then I can remember it being pulled down, and going with my lake-lasses (companions) to see the foundation-stone of the new one laid." . . .

"What was the Hollow like then, Martha?"

"Different to what it is now; but I can tell of it clean different again, when there was neither mill, nor cot, nor hall, except Fieldhead, within two miles of it. I can tell, one summer evening, fifty years syne, my mother coming running in just at the edge of dark, almost fleyed out of her wits, saying she had seen a fairish (fairy) in Fieldhead Hollow; and that was the last fairish that ever was seen on this countryside (though they've been heard within these forty years). A lonesome spot it was, and a bonnie spot, full of oak-trees and nut-trees. It is altered now."'

(*Shirley*, Chapter 37)

From that to the landscape Erskine Stuart saw in 1888 and on to the M62. 'This world has queer changes.'

10. Fame, Fate and Finale

Charlotte – the Richmond Portrait.

Shirley appeared in October 1849, and though it received some critical reviews, it was clear that 'Currer Bell' was now an established novelist. The pseudonym could not hide the author's real identity for long. Indeed, *Shirley* with its local references helped to reveal the facts. The servants at the parsonage were soon telling Charlotte of the conjecture that was going around.

As her fame spread, visitors began to descend on Haworth. One such was the nearby squire, Sir James Kay-Shuttleworth of Gawthorpe Hall, Padiham, who persuaded Charlotte to stay with him and his wife for a week in March 1850. Most of June she spent in London after an earlier visit in late November and early December in 1849. On both occasions she stayed with George Smith, her publisher and his mother at their new house, 76 Gloucester Terrace, Hyde Park Gardens. In July she spent a few days with them in Edinburgh. In August she was visiting at Briery Close, the Windermere home of the Kay-Shuttleworths, and there she met Mrs Gaskell for the first time. She was back in the Lake District with Harriet Martineau at the Knoll, Ambleside in early December.

Eighteen fifty-one was less hectic, but there was another stay with the Smiths for most of June and from them for her first visit to the Gaskells in Manchester. Over the winter of 1851–2 she was afflicted with a variety of illnesses and she also began the writing of *Villette*. In late May and early June 1852 she went alone to Filey and also visited Scarborough. She was back once more with the Smiths in January 1853 for the publication of her latest novel. In April she stayed with the Gaskells once again; and in September Mrs Gaskell returned the visit. In May 1854 Charlotte paid another and final visit to Manchester.

These were the years of fame that came too late—and came, anyway, not always welcome to the shy, retiring young woman that Charlotte was. But she did enjoy London. On her first visit to her publishers Smith, Elder, George Smith took her to the opera, the General Post Office, the House of Commons and the Royal Academy where she saw Landseer's portrait of her hero Wellington on the battlefield of Waterloo. Smith went one better by taking Charlotte to the Chapel Royal where the white-haired, hook-nosed old Duke appeared in person at Morning Prayer on Sunday. Smith also persuaded her to have her portrait painted by Richmond. Margot Peters describes it well:

> 'With its wide-set eyes, broad, intellectual forehead, wistful, rather crooked smile, and firm chin, the smooth brown hair parted in the middle and drawn back loosely over the ears *en bandeau*.'
>
> (*Unquiet Heart*, 1977 edn, p 297)

Smith not only showed her the sights of London; he invited people to meet her as well. She met George Henry Lewes who had reviewed *Shirley* critically. She met another of her heroes, Thackeray, but both then and later their relationship was an uneasy one. His sardonic jesting both offended and increased her seriousness; but he invited her and Smith to dinner, and there she met the Carlyles and Thackeray's friend, Mrs Brookfield.

That evening was a resounding failure, so much so that to the observer at this distance of time it has a touch of the macabre comic about it, as one contemplates the unease of the guests:

> 'It was a gloomy and silent evening. Everyone waited for the brilliant conversation which never began at all. Miss Brontë retired to a sofa in the study, and murmured a word now and then to our kind governess, Miss Truelock. The room looked very dark, the lamp began to smoke a little, the conversation grew dimmer and more dim, the ladies sat round still expectant, my father was too much perturbed by the gloom and the silence to be able to cope with it at all. Mrs Brookfield, who was in the doorway by the study, near the corner in which Miss Brontë was sitting, leant forward with a little commonplace, since brilliance was not to be the order of the evening. "Do you like London, Miss Brontë?" she said; another silence, a pause, then Miss Brontë answers, "Yes and No," very gravely.
>
> ... One day Mrs Procter asked me if I knew what had happened once when my father had invited a party to meet Jane Eyre at his house. It was one of the dullest evenings she had ever spent in her life, she said. And then with a good deal of humour, she described the situation—the ladies who had all come expecting so much

delightful conversation, and the gloom, and the constraint, and how, finally overwhelmed by the situation, my father had quietly left the room, left the house, and gone off to his club.'
(Anne T Ritchie, *Chapters from Some Memoirs*, 1894, pp 60, 65)

Charlotte was back in London in 1851, visiting the Great Exhibition five times and by the last rather bored with it. She found Thackeray's lectures on the English humorists of the eighteenth century more interesting, but she did not appreciate his singling her out and introducing her to his mother as 'Jane Eyre', especially as there were those around to overhear. He paid for it the next day when George Smith 'found a scene in full progress':

'Only these two were in the room. Thackeray was standing on the hearth-rug, looking anything but happy. Charlotte Brontë stood close to him, with head thrown back and face white with anger. The first words I heard were, "No Sir! If *you* had come to our part of the country in Yorkshire, what would you have thought of me if I had introduced you to my father, before a mixed company of strangers, as 'Mr Warrington'?" Thackeray replied, "No, you mean 'Arthur Pendennis'." "No, I *don't* mean Arthur Pendennis!" retorted Miss Brontë. "I mean Mr Warrington, and Mr Warrington would not have behaved as you behaved to me yesterday." The spectacle of this little woman, hardly reaching to Thackeray's elbow, but, somehow looking stronger and fiercer than himself, and casting her incisive words at his head, resembled the dropping of shells into a fortress.'
(Sidney Lee, *George Smith: A Memoir*, 1902, pp 99–100)

Thackeray turned out for Charlotte a god with brazen feet. He was too much attracted by that society whose superficialities and hypocrisies he had himself both vividly recognized and ruthlessly exposed.

On the 1851 visit Charlotte went to the theatre to see the famous actress Rachel, and she also went to hear Cardinal Wiseman whose performance she found no less theatrical, 'impiously theatrical' she called it. She ministered to her father's vehement anti-Catholicism (and perhaps, after Brussels, to her own) when she described the scene to him in a letter of 17 June 1851:

'He came swimming into the room smiling, simpering, and bowing like a fat old lady, and sat down very demure in his chair, and looked the picture of a sleek hypocrite. He was dressed in black like a bishop or dean in plain clothes, but wore scarlet gloves and a brilliant scarlet waistcoat. A bevy of inferior priests surrounded him, many of them very dark-looking and sinister men. The Cardinal spoke in a smooth whining manner, just like a canting Methodist preacher. The audience seemed to look up to him as to a god. A spirit of the hottest zeal pervaded the whole meeting.'

During these years of fame Charlotte had maintained her friendship with and visits to and from Ellen Nussey. The Nusseys had moved from Rydings to a house not far away on the hillside, Brookroyd, and it was there that Charlotte was staying when *Shirley* was published. It was appropriate that she should be in the district in which it was set. The anonymity she had sought as an author was now cracking. Ellen had been told under a vow of silence, but others made inferences and reached conclusions, not always favourable, be it said. Writing to W S Williams of the house of Smith, Elder on 1 November 1849, she declared:

> 'During my late visit I have too often had reason, sometimes in a pleasant, sometimes in a painful form, to fear that I no longer walk invisible. *Jane Eyre*, it appears, has been read all over the district — a fact of which I never dreamt — I met sometimes with new deference, with augmented kindness: old schoolfellows and old teachers, too, greeted me with generous warmth. And, again, ecclesiastical brows lowered thunder at me.'

Brookroyd is part of the Brontë landscape, the least remarkable part in itself. As long ago as 1888 Erskine Stuart asserted that 'no particular interest attaches to the building, so we will dismiss this in a word.' Since then, surrounded by small modern dwellings, it has acquired the most unimpressive stucco and more recently a plastic canopy over the front door.

Besides her literary occupations Charlotte had to look after her father whose declining years and declining eyesight provided increasing trials. In 1846 she had taken him to Manchester for a cataract operation. Charlotte had to bear this burden and greater suffering alone, for her fame, and in its lesser degree her sisters' fame, had come too late for them to enjoy it. In a letter to William Smith Williams, Charlotte wrote on 13 June 1849:

> 'A year ago — had a prophet warned me how I should stand in June 1849 — how stripped and bereaved — had he foretold the autumn, the winter, the spring of sickness and suffering to be gone through — I should have thought this can never be endured. It is over. Branwell — Emily — Anne are gone like dreams — gone as Maria and Elizabeth went twenty years ago. One by one I watched them fall

asleep on my arm—and closed their glazed eyes—I have seen them buried one by one—and thus far—God has upheld me. From my heart I thank Him.'

She was alone. All were gone. It is touching to note that even at the distance of two decades the then younger and smaller sister remembered the older ones, those little older ones, whom she so much loved and revered.

The nearer sorrows, however, were yet greater afflictions. By 1848 Branwell's wild career had run its course. His last months were horror, filled with suicidal and homicidal threat. He slept in his father's bedroom and the sisters spent each night in fearful wondering as to what might happen. The end came on 24 September 1848. Charlotte wrote to Ellen:

'A deep conviction that he rests at last—rests well after his brief, erring, suffering, feverish life—fills and quiets my mind now. The final separation, the spectacle of his pale corpse, gave me more acute bitter pain than I could have imagined. Till the last hour comes, we never know how much we can forgive, pity, regret a near relative. All his vices were and are nothing now. We remember only his woes.'

Emily went next and went quickly but, in the characteristic fashion of her indomitable spirit, she did not 'go gentle into that good night'. Here is Charlotte again from the biographical notice of her sisters:

'Day by day, when I saw with what a front she met suffering, I looked on her with an anguish of wonder and love. I have seen nothing like it; but, indeed I have never seen her parallel in anything. Stronger than a man, simpler than a child, her nature stood alone. . . . While full of ruth for others, on her self she had no pity; the spirit was inexorable to the flesh; from the trembling hands, the unnerved limbs, the fading eyes, the same service was exacted as they had rendered in health.'

Racked by the coughing and emaciation of tuberculosis, Emily refused to give in. Charlotte searched Emily's beloved moors for 'a lingering spray of heather—just one spray, however withered'; she took it in and 'saw that the flower was not recognized by the dim and indifferent eyes.' Yet Emily insisted on getting up and she insisted on not having a doctor. She got up on Tuesday, 19 December 1848 and at last agreed to medical help. She was dead by two o'clock in the afternoon. Her fierce old dog, Keeper, accompanied the mourners into the church and then howled pitifully at

Anne's grave in the churchyard of St Mary's, Scarborough; Charlotte visited it in 1852, while staying at Filey.

Inscription indicating Anne's grave.

Emily's bedroom door for days afterwards.

As Mrs Gaskell puts it, 'Anne Brontë drooped and sickened more rapidly from that time.' She too died exactly in character; she did go gentle into that good night. Always delicate, she declined over months delicately towards her end. Charlotte knew: 'Anne's decline is gradual and fluctuating; but its nature is not in doubt.' May arrived, and Charlotte and Ellen Nussey took Anne to Scarborough, a place where she had been when she was governess with the Robinsons. What she must have suffered on that journey! They travelled on 24 May; she died on the 28th. There is something still more pathetic in her end, for she died away from home, and she alone is buried apart from the rest of her family. Dear gentle Anne rests separate in the churchyard at St Mary's, Scarborough. That was why on her visit to Filey in 1852 Charlotte went also to Scarborough—to see the grave and gravestone of her last loved sister.

Charlotte described how she felt about her sisters' deaths. Writing to Williams on 4 June 1849, she told him first of Anne:

> 'She died without severe struggle, resigned, trusting in God— thankful for release from a suffering life—deeply assured that a better existence lay before her. She believed, she hoped—and declared her belief and hope with her last breath. Her quiet, Christian death did not rend my heart as Emily's stern, simple undemonstrative end did. I let Anne go to God, and felt He had a right to her. I could hardly let Emily go. I wanted to hold her back then, and I want her back now. Anne, from her childhood, seemed preparing for an early death. Emily's spirit seemed strong enough to bear her to fulness of years. They are both gone, and so is poor Branwell, and Papa has now me only—the weakest, puniest, least promising of his six children.'

She ends that letter:

> 'I have heard from Papa. He and the servants knew when they parted from Anne they would see her no more. All tried to be resigned. I knew it likewise, and I wanted her to die where she would be happiest. She loved Scarbro'. A peaceful sun gilded her evening.'

Charlotte returned home from burying Anne. Her mood was a mixture of deep sorrow and loneliness on the one hand and, on the other, that strange exalting faith that the Christian finds in bereavement:

> 'I tried to be glad that I was come home. I have always been glad

before—except once—even then I was cheered. But this time joy was not to be the sensation. I felt that the house was all silent—the rooms were all empty. I remembered where the three were laid—in what narrow dark dwellings—never more to reappear on earth. So the sense of desolation and bitterness took possession of me. The agony that *was to be undergone,* and *was not* to be avoided, came on. I underwent it, and passed a dreary evening and night, and a mournful morrow; today I am better.

I do not know how life will pass, but I certainly do feel confidence in Him who has upheld me hitherto. Solitude may be cheered, and made endurable beyond what I can believe.'

(*Life*, Chapter 17)

That letter contains also a particularly pathetic touch:

'The dogs seemed in strange ecstasy. I am certain they regarded me as the harbinger of others. The dumb creatures thought that as I was returned, those who had been so long absent were not far behind.'

The dogs, and especially Keeper, deserve more than passing mention. He survived till near the end of 1851:

'He had come to the Parsonage in the fierce strength of his youth. Sullen and ferocious he had met with his master in the indomitable Emily. Like most dogs of his kind, he feared, respected, and deeply loved her who subdued him. He had mourned her with the pathetic fidelity of his nature, falling into old age after her death. And now, [Charlotte] wrote: "Poor old Keeper died last Monday morning, after being ill one night; he went gently to sleep; we laid his old faithful head in the garden. Flossy (the 'fat curly-haired dog') is dull, and misses him. There was something very sad in losing the old dog; yet I am glad he met a natural fate. People kept hinting he ought to be put away, which neither papa nor I liked to think of."'

(*Life*, Chapter 24)

After her sisters' deaths Charlotte was left alone with her father. The selfish old man, as Mary Taylor had years before so acutely discerned him to be, did not improve with the years. But Charlotte, had she so wished, might by now have married. In 1839 she had refused an offer by Ellen Nussey's brother, Henry, whom some, including Mrs Gaskell, have improbably seen as at least a partial model for St John Rivers in *Jane Eyre*. Henry Nussey had none of that character's heroism. He had been rejected by one lady two days before he proposed to Charlotte. Rejected

in turn by her, he recorded in his diary, 'Received an unfavourable reply
from CB. The Will of the Lord be done.' Not much passion there! He was
eventually accepted by a parishioner of Charles Kingsley's, Emily
Prescott of Eversley (Hampshire). Her wealth did not make for happiness
and they eventually parted, Henry going to live in the South of France. It
took only one visit and a few days for Charlotte to receive another
proposal (in August 1839) from a forward young Irish curate from Colne,
one David Bryce, who, like Willie Weightman, was to meet an early death
some few months later.

'Marriage', said Mrs Gaskell, 'did not enter into the scheme of her
life.' The matter, however, is worth more exploration than that.
Charlotte wrote to Ellen Nussey about Henry's proposal on 12 March
1839:

> 'I asked myself two questions: Do I love him as much as a woman
> ought to love the man she marries? Am I the person best qualified to
> make him happy? Alas! Ellen, my conscience answered *no* to both
> these questions .... I had not, and could not have, that intense
> attachment that would make me willing to die for him; and if ever I
> marry, it must be in that light of adoration that I will regard my
> husband.'

Plenty of passion there, passion indeed of the sort that distinguishes Jane
Eyre's reaction to Rochester as compared with that to St John Rivers,
passion that involves, over all else, sacrifice.

Other proposals came her way; and she may have been interested in
one from whom no proposal came, George Smith. In 1844, however,
someone else appeared on the scene, her father's latest curate, Arthur Bell
Nicholls, yet another of that plenteous brood of Irishmen who seem to
have been making their way in the Church in Yorkshire at that time.
There were rumours, rumours, Charlotte assured Ellen Nussey in a letter
of 10 July 1846, 'never ... more unfounded .... A cold faraway sort of
civility are the only terms on which I have ever been with Mr Nicholls.'
Eight years later (!) Nicholls proposed to Charlotte. We have the account
not only of hers but also her father's reaction, as she gave it to Ellen
Nussey (15 December 1852):

> 'After tea I withdrew to the dining-room as usual. As usual, Mr
> Nicholls sat with papa till between eight and nine o'clock, I then
> heard him open the parlour door as if going. I expected the clash of
> the front door. He stopped in the passage: he tapped: like lightning
> it flashed on me what was coming. He entered—he stood before me.
> What his words were you can guess; his manner—you can hardly

Arthur Bell Nicholls, the curate whom Charlotte married in 1854 and who, returning to Ireland on Patrick's death in 1861, survived her for over fifty years.

Marriage certificate of Arthur Bell Nicholls and Charlotte Brontë, 29 June 1854.

realise—never can I forget it. Shaking from head to foot, looking deadly pale, speaking low, vehemently yet with difficulty—he made me for the first time feel what it costs a man to declare affection where he doubts response.

The spectacle of one ordinarily so statue-like, thus trembling, stirred, and overcome, gave me a kind of strange shock. He spoke of sufferings he had borne for months, of sufferings he could endure no longer, and craved leave for some hope. I could only entreat him to

The Brontë Waterfall on Haworth Moor – 'a perfect torrent raving over the rocks'.

leave me then and promise a reply on the morrow. I asked him if he had spoken to papa. He said, he dared not. I think I half led, half put him out of the room. When he was gone I immediately went to papa, and told him what had taken place. Agitation and anger disproportionate to the occasion ensued; if I had *loved* Mr Nicholls and had heard such epithets applied to him as were used, it would have transported me past my patience; as it was, my blood boiled with a sense of injustice, but papa worked himself into a state not to be trifled with, the veins on his temples started up like whipcord, and his eyes became suddenly bloodshot. I made haste to promise that Mr Nicholls should on the morrow have a distinct refusal.

I wrote yesterday and got his note. There is no need to add to this statement any comment. Papa's vehement antipathy to the bare thought of any one thinking of me as a wife, and Mr Nicholls's distress, both give me pain. Attachment to Mr Nicholls you are aware I never entertained, but the poignant pity inspired by his state on Monday evening, by the hurried revelation of his sufferings for many months, is something galling and irksome. That he cared something for me, and wanted me to care for him, I have long suspected, but I did not know the degree or strength of his feelings. Dear Nell, goodbye.'

There was near-pandemonium. Patrick Brontë wrote Nicholls an insulting letter. Nicholls resigned his curacy, withdrew his resignation, and had the withdrawal accepted by Patrick only on condition that marriage be never mentioned again. Nicholls in despair thought of going to Australia but eventually settled for a curacy at Kirk Smeaton (near Pontefract). Charlotte continued to correspond with him. Patrick Brontë's new curate, de Renzi, was a disaster. Nicholls returned in May 1854 as curate once again and as husband-to-be.

On the eve of the marriage (on 29 June 1854) Patrick decided he was too unwell—more accurately perhaps, too peevish and ill-tempered—to attend. Charlotte had to be given away by Miss Wooler. The honeymoon was spent in Ireland, visiting Nicholls' relatives, staying in the family home, Cuba House, Banagher, then on to a tour of the west and south of Ireland. Sir James Kay-Shuttleworth reappeared and offered Nicholls the living of Padiham, but he and Charlotte were resolute not to leave her father.

Nicholls was a conventional character, lacking both in the breadth of mind and the tolerance of spirit that one might have expected in Charlotte's husband. She, now nearing forty, had made a considered judgement in accepting him. She found him authoritarian and possessive, but she found him also devoted and affectionate. Their joy was not to last long, blighted like almost everything about the Brontës.

They went for a walk on the moors in late November 1854:

'When we had got about half a mile on the moors, Arthur suggested the idea of the waterfall—after the melted snow he said it would be fine .... It was fine indeed—a perfect torrent raving over the rocks, white and beautiful. It began to rain while we were watching it, and we returned home under a stormy sky.'

(Letter to Ellen Nussey, 29 November 1854)

Charlotte caught cold. This was accentuated by a long walk on damp ground in thin shoes when they visited Gawthorpe in the new year. She was overcome with nausea and faintness, the consequences possibly of early pregnancy. To add to all this, faithful old Tabby died suddenly in February. Charlotte's condition worsened. In her husband she found 'the tenderest nurse, the kindest support, the best earthly comfort that woman ever had.' Looking at him desperately, she whispered, 'Oh! I am not going to die, am I? He will not separate us, we have been so happy.'

She was and He did. The last of the six Brontë children breathed her last on the last day of March 1855. Their names are recorded on the plaque in the Brontë chapel of St Michael and All Angels, Haworth, the premature deaths—all but one and he the sire—of the ill-fated members of this sad family.

The Brontë Memorial Plaque on the wall of the Brontë Chapel in Haworth Church.

Nicholls was to stay with the old man until Patrick himself died. On that Saturday morning of 31 March 1855:

'. . . the solemn tolling of Haworth church bell spoke forth the fact of [Charlotte's] death to the villagers who had known her from a child, and whose hearts shivered within them as they thought of the two sitting, desolate and alone in the old grey house.'

(Life, Chapter 27)

So Mrs Gaskell. No other words are necessary because none could better them.

The Brontë Chapel in the south-east corner of Haworth Church, the Brontë Memorial clearly visible. The chapel was dedicated in 1964, and includes a memorial window donated by an American admirer.

Chronology

1777 17 March Patrick Brontë born at Drumballyroney, County Down, Ireland.
1783 Maria Branwell born at Penzance, Cornwall.
1802–6 Patrick at St John's College, Cambridge. Graduated BA.
1806 Curate of Wethersfield, Essex.
1809 Curate of Wellington, Shropshire. Curate of Dewsbury.
1811 Curate of Hartshead.
1812 Patrick and Maria Branwell meet at Woodhouse Grove School, Apperley Bridge. Married at Guiseley Church, 29 December.
1814 January Birth of Maria Brontë.
1815 8 February Birth of Elizabeth Brontë.
1815 Patrick becomes incumbent of Thornton.
1816 21 April Charlotte born at Thornton.
1817 26 June Patrick Branwell born at Thornton.
1818 30 July Emily Jane born at Thornton.
1820 17 January Anne born at Thornton.
February Patrick becomes incumbent of Haworth.
1821 25 September Mrs Brontë dies. Her sister, Elizabeth ('Aunt Branwell'), arrives to look after the family.
1823 Patrick's proposals for remarriage rejected.
1824 July Maria and Elizabeth go to Cowan Bridge School.
August Charlotte follows, and Emily in November.
1825 14 February Maria left, ill—died 6 May.
31 May Elizabeth left, ill—died 15 June.
1 June Patrick brings Charlotte and Emily home. Tabitha Aykroyd joins the Brontë household.
1826 The 'little writings' begin.
1831 January Charlotte goes to Roe Head, meets Ellen Nussey and Mary Taylor.
1832 July Charlotte leaves Roe Head.
September Charlotte makes her first visit to Ellen Nussey's home, Rydings, Birstall.
1833 July Ellen Nussey stays at Haworth.
1835 July Charlotte returns to Roe Head as teacher. Emily comes as pupil, but leaves after two months. Anne replaces her and stays till December 1837. Branwell goes to study at the Royal Academy but returns penniless after a few days. Later (1838) sets up as portrait painter in Bradford, but is unsuccessful.

1837 October Emily goes to Law Hill near Halifax as teacher but soon returns home.
1838 May Charlotte leaves Miss Wooler's school.
1839 March Charlotte receives marriage proposal from Henry Nussey, and in August from James Bryce.
April Anne goes to Mrs Ingram, Blake Hall, Mirfield as governess and leaves in December.
May Charlotte goes to Mrs Sidgwick, Stonegappe, Lothersdale as governess and leaves in July.
August William Weightman comes as curate to Haworth (dies September 1842).
September Charlotte and Ellen Nussey visit Bridlington.
1840 January Branwell becomes tutor to the Postlethwaite boys at Barrow-in-Furness but leaves in June.
March Anne goes as governess to Mrs Robinson, Thorp Green, Little Ouseburn, near York.
September Branwell is railway clerk at Luddendenfoot, then at Sowerby Bridge (April 1841), but dismissed (April 1842).
1841 March Charlotte goes as governess to Mrs White, Upperwood, Rawdon, but leaves in December.
1842 February Charlotte and Emily go to Heger School in Brussels, but return on Aunt Branwell's death in October.
1843 January Charlotte returns to Brussels alone. Branwell goes with Anne to Thorp Green as tutor.
1844 January Charlotte comes back to Haworth.
August Arthur Bell Nicholls becomes curate at Haworth.
1845 June Anne leaves Thorp Green.
July Branwell dismissed from Thorp Green. Family all at home. Charlotte stays with Ellen Nussey at Hathersage.
1846 May *Poems* by Currer, Ellis and Acton Bell.
1847 October *Jane Eyre* published by Smith, Elder. December *Wuthering Heights* and *Agnes Grey* published by Newby.
1848 July Charlotte and Anne visit Smith, Elder to prove their separate identity. *The Tenant of Wildfell Hall* published by Newby.
24 September Death of Branwell.

19 December Death of Emily.
1849 28 May Death of Anne.
June Charlotte stays at Bridlington again.
October *Shirley* published.
November-December Charlotte stays in London with George Smith and his mother.
1850 March Visits the Kay-Shuttleworths at Gawthorpe.
June In London again. Dinner party at Thackeray's house. Richmond paints her portrait.
July Visits Edinburgh with the Smiths.
August Stays with the Kay-Shuttleworths at Briery Close, Windermere and meets Mrs Gaskell.
1851 May-June Visits the Great Exhibition in London and hears Thackeray lecture.
June Stays with the Gaskells in Manchester.
1852 May-June Visit to Filey and Anne's grave at Scarborough.
December *Villette* published. Nicholls' proposal of marriage. Violent objections from Patrick Brontë. Nicholls goes as curate to Kirk Smeaton in May 1853.

1853 January Last visit to London.
April Spends a week with the Gaskells in Manchester. Mrs Gaskell returns the visit in September.
1854 April Engagement to Arthur Bell Nicholls.
May Nicholls returns to Haworth as curate.
29 June Marriage. Miss Wooler gave Charlotte away; Ellen Nussey bridesmaid. Honeymoon in Ireland (Dublin, Cork, Killarney and Nicholls' house at Banagher).
1855 January Visit to Kay-Shuttleworths at Gawthorpe. Charlotte catches cold.
31 March Charlotte dies.
1857 Mrs Gaskell's *Life of Charlotte Brontë*. *The Professor* (Charlotte's first novel) published.
1861 7 June Death of Patrick Brontë. Nicholls returns to Ireland.

Useful Addresses

The Brontë Parsonage Museum,
Haworth,
Keighley,
West Yorkshire

The following are all open to the public:
Gawthorpe Hall,
Padiham,
Lancashire

Norton Conyers,
Ripon,
Yorkshire

Oakwell Hall,
Nutter Lane,
Birstall,
Nr Batley,
Yorkshire

Red House,
Gomersal,
Nr Cleckheaton,
West Yorkshire

Bibliography

Writings
The **novels** are readily available in various editions, of which the most authoritative is the Clarendon (Oxford) with publication still proceeding. There is no up-to-date standard edition of the **poems**, but the following may be consulted:-

The Poems of Charlotte and Patrick Branwell Brontë (Shakespeare Head, Blackwell, 1934)
The Poems of Patrick Branwell Brontë ed T Winnifrith (Shakespeare Head, Blackwell, 1983)
The Poems of Emily Jane and Anne Brontë (Shakespeare Head, Blackwell, 1934)
The Poems of Anne Brontë ed E Chitham (Macmillan, 1979)
The Complete Poems of Emily Brontë ed C W Hatfield (Oxford and Columbia University Presses, 1941)

The **early work** can be sampled in:-
An Edition of the Early Writings of Charlotte Brontë, 1826–32 ed C Alexander (Shakespeare Head, Blackwell, 1987)
Five Novelettes (by Charlotte Brontë) ed W Gérin (Folio Society, 1971)
Legends of Angria ed F E Ratchford and W C de Vane (York University Press, 1933)

The **letters** are to be found in the comprehensive, but not always reliable:-
The Brontës: Their Lives, Friendships and Correspondence ed T J Wise and J A Symington, 4 Vols (Shakespeare Head, Blackwell, 1932)

Also:-
The Brontës: Life and Letters ed C K Shorter, 2 Vols (Hodder and Stoughton, 1908)

Biography
Gaskell, E C, *Life of Charlotte Brontë* 3 Vols (Smith, Elder, 1857)
Gérin, W, *Anne Brontë* revised edition (Nelson, 1975)
— *Branwell Brontë* (Nelson, 1961)
— *Charlotte Brontë: The Evolution of Genius* (Clarendon Press, 1966)
— *Emily Brontë* (Clarendon Press, 1971)
Hanson, L and EM, *The Four Brontës* (Oxford University Press, 1949; revised, 1967)
Lane, M, *The Brontë Story: A Reconsideration of Mrs Gaskell's Life of Charlotte Brontë* (Heinemann, 1953)
Lock, J, and W T Dixon, *A Man of Sorrow: The Life, Letters and Times of the Rev Patrick Brontë* (Nelson, 1965)
Peters, M, *Unquiet Soul: A Biography of Charlotte Brontë* (Hodder and Stoughton, 1975)

Criticism

Alexander, C, *The Early Writings of Charlotte Brontë* (Blackwell, 1983)

Allott, M, ed *The Brontës: The Critical Heritage* (Routledge and Kegan Paul, 1974)

Craik, W A, *The Brontë Novels* (Methuen, 1968)

Ewbank, I-S, *Their Proper Sphere: A Study of the Brontë Sisters as Early Victorian Female Novelists* (Arnold, 1966)

Martin, R B, *The Accents of Persuasion* (Faber and Faber, 1966)

Ratchford, F E, *The Brontës' Web of Childhood* (Columbia University Press, 1941)

Winnifrith, T J, *The Brontës and Their Background* (Macmillan, 1973)

Topography

Chadwick, E H, *In the Footsteps of the Brontës* (Pitman, 1914)

Erskine Stuart, J, *The Brontë Country* (Longmans, 1888)

Horsfall Turner, J, *Haworth Past and Present* (J S Jowett, 1879; reprinted, Otley, Olicare Books, 1971)

Kellett, J, *Haworth Parsonage: The Home of the Brontës* (The Brontë Society, Haworth, 1977)

Wroot, H E, *The Persons and Places of the Brontë Novels* (Brontë Society Transactions, Vol III, 1906; reprinted and enlarged, Outhwaite Bros, Shipley, 1935)

General

Lloyd Evans, G and B, *Everyman's Companion to the Brontës* (Dent, 1982)

Transactions of the Brontë Society, annually since 1895; to be published twice yearly from 1987 (The Brontë Society, Haworth)

Index

ACKNOWLEDGEMENTS

The author and publisher would like to thank the following for their help: The Incorporated Brontë Society (Brontë Parsonage Museum); Sir James Graham (Norton Conyers); Kirklees Libraries, Museums and Arts, Kirklees Metropolitan Council (Oakwell Hall, Red House Museum); The National Trust (Gawthorpe Hall); the Supervisor (Roe Head School); St John's College, Cambridge.
And for permission to redraw maps: Bradford Libraries and Information Service (map of Haworth); Stanley Chapman (map of Shirley Country).

The publishers would like to thank the following for supplying illustrations:
Black and white:
Calverley Parish Church 37; Casterton School, Kirkby Lonsdale 58; The Incorporated Brontë Society 9, 23, 39 above and below, 41, 42 above and below, 43, 61, 75, 77, 79, 137, 141, 159, 182 above and below; Simon McBride frontispiece, 10–11, 14–5, 18, 19, 21, 24, 30 above and below, 33, 34, 35, 38, 44, 49, 50–1, 53, 56, 57, 62, 63, 70–1, 80–1, 82–3, 84, 92–3, 95, 97, 99, 100–101, 110, 117, 120, 121, 122, 130–1, 133, 150, 151, 152–3, 161, 162 above and below, 178 above and below, 183, 185, 186; National Portrait Gallery 8, 173.

Colour:
The Incorporated Brontë Society 45 below left and right; Simon McBride 25 above and below, 26–7, 28, 45 above, 46–7, 48 above and below, 65 above and below, 66, 67 above and below, 68 above and below, 85 above and below, 86–7, 87 above and below, 88 above and below, 105, 106–7, 108 above and below, 125 above and below, 126 above and below, 127, 128 above and below, 145, 146–7, 148 above and below, 166–7, 168; by courtesy of the National Trust 165 above and below.

Every endeavour has been made to trace the copyright holders of the following: 103, 157.

Maps on 16 and 171 drawn by Malcolm Couch.